DEVELOPING AND MANAGING VIDEO COLLECTIONS

anual for

on

*HOW-TO-DO-IT MANUALS
FOR LIBRARIES*

NUMBER 68

NEAL-SCHUMAN PUBLISHERS, INC.
New York, London

Published by Neal-Schuman Publishers, Inc.
100 Varick Street
New York, NY 10013

Printed and bound in the United States of America.

Library of Congress Cataloging-in-Publication Data

Mason-Robinson, Sally.
   Developing and managing video collections : a how-to-do-it manual
for librarians / by Sally Mason-Robinson.
      p.   cm—(How-to-do-it manuals for librarians ; 68)
   Includes bibliographical references and index.
   ISBN 1-55570-230-9
   1. Libraries—United States—Special collections—Video
recordings. I. Title. II. Series: How-to-do-it manuals for libraries ;
no. 68.
Z692.V52M37   1996
025.2'873—dc20   96-3058

For Wylie

ACKNOWLEDGMENTS

We are fortunate in the library media field to have such collegial working conditions. There are a number of wonderful, generous people who have helped me synthesize my thoughts. First and foremost, thanks to my friend Irene Wood, whose professionalism and humor have helped for more years than either of us cares to discuss; also, thanks to Jim Scholtz, Randy Pitman, Pat Lora, Gary Handman, Jean Kreamer, and that mentor-of-mentors, Margaret Chisholm. I'm grateful to Lucie Singh for keeping the trains running on time, and to Debra Franco for holding the light. A special thank you to Joseph Rice at the Chicago Public Library for being an excellent reference librarian and sounding board.

I also want to recognize National Video Resources and the John D. and Catherine T. MacArthur Foundation for their support of projects that have helped us keep the faith and carry the torch.

Lastly, thank you to all the dedicated, inspiring librarians who deliver excellent service, often against enormous odds.

CONTENTS

PREFACE

*"It is my firm conviction that a large part
of education in coming generations will be
not by books but by motion pictures."*
— Thomas Alva Edison, 1923

I wrote *Developing and Managing Video Collections in Libraries: A How-To-Do-It Manual* to help librarians deal with those aspects of collection development and management that are unique to the video format. It is designed for two kinds of readers: librarians who are significantly expanding existing video collections—or building brand new ones—can use the book as a blueprint for going from developing policies as well as acquiring, circulating, and preserving high-quality appropriate titles which will attract new users to the library. Librarians seeking to solve a specific problem or expand their knowledge about a particular aspect of video collection development and management (whether that is developing a selection policy or how to arrange video shelving) can consult individual sections or chapters of the book for advice and guidance.

A LITTLE HISTORY

In order to understand how video has gotten to be such an integral part of library service, it's helpful to look at its growth. The library system I was working for in 1970 decided to renovate a library branch I was then supervising. A member of the library's advisory council was something of a visionary and insisted that the branch be wired to receive cable television signals. Though it was an innovative plan, there was a feeling among the technologically tuned-in that cable television was "just around the corner." At the same time, we all talked about the coming revolution in videotape technology, and oohed-and-ahed at the sleek new 3/4" reel-to-reel video player.

While we suspected that video would revolutionize library audiovisual service in some way, I don't think any of us could foresee the home video phenomenon that finally took place in the mid-1980s. If I can recall what I thought then, I believe it was that the library's 16mm film collection would be made available on tape, which would cut down on inspection and repair. Today we take for granted that video is a part of all types of library service, providing both essential research materials and popular entertainment.

The point is that the more things change, the more they stay the same. Here in the mid-1990s, we are looking at another "technological revolution," though, admittedly, this one is of breathtaking vastness. While we know that the delivery and reception of visual information is changing, and while we have some ideas about what the future might look like, we really can't know how it will turn out. The one "sure bet," however, is that the 1/2" VHS videocassette will be with us for some time to come. It is the medium of choice for the delivery of motion pictures in the home, educational, and community institutions. Today, more than 80 percent of American households boast *at least* one videocassette player. In 1987, that number was only 50 percent. [1]

FROM FILM TO VIDEO

While film service had been a part of a good public library's collection since the 1950s, film collections tended to be found only in large urban libraries, library systems, and wealthier suburban communities. The truth of the matter is that film was really an elite service which few people in the community could access, except through public library screenings. Though film service was admittedly limited in its scope, the tremendous contribution these collections made in their communities cannot be overstated. Then, as now, the public library was *the* source for a wonderful array of creative and informative work not readily available anywhere else. The public library was the main outlet for the works of independent filmmakers, social documentarians, film artists, biographers, and animators. The audience for these works, while never vast in mass-media terms, was nevertheless steady and enthusiastic. These library collections served community groups (who were, by and large, the only owners of 16mm projectors) such as youth groups, religious institutions, senior centers, as well as interest groups formed around various issues and causes.

Film programming was both a service and an art. Libraries ran in-house film programs. While story hours have always been a main platform for film programming, films were also used in young adult, travel, social issue, and senior citizen programs. Some libraries were also pioneers in presenting film artists both showing and discussing their works.

The relationship between the library and the filmmaker was symbiotic. While the market for the films was never huge, it was steady. Filmmakers could count on a certain number of sales for a good price. Library audiovisual specialists became the community experts in film programming. Let me hasten to add to this idyllic picture, however, that nobody got rich. Filmmakers were consider fortunate to make enough to finance their next project. Libraries, ever vulnerable to the economy's vagaries, suffered from periodic budget cuts. And make no mistake, audiovisual *always* got cut first.

In schools and academic institutions, the situation was somewhat different than in public libraries. Large publishers such as McGraw-Hill and Britannica, led the way in creating the instructional films that became a part of all our childhoods. Without looking too closely at the quality of most of these presentations as films, they certainly were a part of almost every classroom. Academic libraries also had long-established collections and led the way in collecting and archiving alternative and challenging films. Additionally, some large universities served as sources for school districts without their own film libraries.

THE VIDEO REVOLUTION

When the video revolution finally did occur, it did so with mindboggling quickness. Sony owned the market in the beginning with their 3/4" reel-to-reel then videocassette formats. They developed the 1/2" Beta format specifically for the home market, then sat back on their laurels and waited. Unfortunately for them their upstart competitor, JVC, had also developed a 1/2" videocassette format. While most video experts agree that as a format VHS has never been of the same quality as Beta, Sony napped while they were soundly beaten in the marketplace by enthusiastic and unremitting promotion and delivery for the VHS format. Coupled with the economic boom of the 1980s, the home video industry took off. Machines flew off retailers' shelves. Video rental stores appeared on every corner. The movie industry, at first extremely wary of what it saw as direct competition to movie ticket sales, found it had a whole new market.

And libraries were presented with an exciting new opportunity. Video was not only new and popular, it was a library service developed from *user* demand. While library staff assigned the daunting duty of the checkout corner on a Friday afternoon might have had trouble remaining enthusiastic through the fatigue of dealing with long lines, it cannot be denied that video opened up library service to whole segments of the community which had never before used the library. At the same time, home use of VHS and off-air taping opened up new opportunities for classroom teachers to offer audiovisual materials without the time-consuming task of booking films and waiting for delivery.

Video collections grew in a couple of different ways. For schools and libraries with 16mm film collections, video was at first just another delivery system for the same content. Policies thus tended to reflect the restrictive practices that were necessary when handling an expensive format like film. Libraries without experience in circulating films turned to the only model available—the local video store. Neither model was what was ultimately needed.

Video has now become a mainstay of library service. Most public libraries report at least 10 percent of their circulation is video, many are in the 20 percent range, and a few report that video is as much as 40 percent of their circulation. Whatever the number, there is no question that "film" has now come of age as a library service.

ABOUT THIS BOOK

For libraries, this exploding growth in collection size and circulation has been both a wonderful opportunity and an incredible challenge. This book's six chapters and five appendices will help librarians deal with those aspects of collection development and management that are unique to the video format.

- Chapter 1, "The Video Collection," examines the similarities and differences between video and other formats. The chapter discusses the ways in which video is a better transmitter of information than print. The chapter also discuses how to establish the breadth and balance of the video collection, including the desirable proportion of non-fiction (informational, documentary, and how-to) and fiction (narrative feature films) videos. Discussions of specific genres such as foreign films, children's videos, and independent films (including tips on where to locate quality programs) are included.
- Chapter 2, "Evaluating Video," covers what is often the most overlooked aspect of building video collections—evaluation. While most librarians have little time for a detailed evaluation of titles, an understanding of what elements comprise a good presentation is essential. Chapter 2 discusses the three main elements librarians should consider when evaluating individual programs: content (organization, presentation of information, and script), technical aspects (such as visuals, sound, and editing) and usage (appropriateness for patrons and suitability for programming). To help facilitate evaluation, I've included a model evaluation form in the appendix.

- Chapter 3, "Selection and Acquisitions," covers all aspects of locating and purchasing videos. Professional review sources, consumer reviews, and useful reference tools are all discussed. I've included several lists such as recommended sleeper films and the best children's videos to both illustrate excellent selection choices and exemplify the uniqueness the library can bring to the public's viewing choices. Background information on the video business and how it impacts library purchasing is also included. Differences between the three types of video sellers (wholesalers, retailers, and single source distributors) are explained. The chapter also looks at how video sellers dovetail with—and differ from—book purchasing outlets. Acquisitions functions, such as staff responsibility for purchasing, off-air taping guidelines, and cooperative and consortia purchasing, are also described.
- Chapter 4, "Collection Development Policies," assists librarians in evaluating their current policies or developing new policies from scratch. Areas covered include those essential for any good collection development policy (from evaluating the constituency to budget, format, and hardware considerations) as well as suggestions for circulation, fee, and interlibrary loan policies. Attention is given to two areas affecting video collections in every library: copyright (particularly public performance rights) and access (including how the MPAA ratings system relates to libraries).
- Chapter 5, "Collection Management," contains the nuts and bolts of day-to-day video service. Cataloging, classification, processing, packaging, shelving, display, security, storage, preservation, weeding, and marketing the collection are all covered.
- When writing the final chapter, "New Technologies and Video Collections," I remembered the 1970 rennovation experience I described at the beginning of this preface. Chapter 6 is perhaps the most important one for library planning purposes because like everything technology touches, so much is changing so quickly in this area. Rather than try to prognosticate (a crystal ball operation at best), this chapter provides readers with the tools they need to make intelligent choices about what may be on the horizon and when (or if) to adopt a specific new format.
- The five appendices present *Booklist*'s criteria for evaluating nonprint materials, a model video collection form, consortium models for purchasing, and those four interpretations of the Library Bill of Rights that are particularly applicable

to video, as well as a list of festivals and awards ceremonies which will help you choose videos in unique categories.

Looking at all these chapters, forms, and lists, it's hard to believe that until just a few years ago it was a joke that if you walked into an unfamiliar library, you never had to ask where the audiovisual department was—you just headed for the basement. Video swiftly moved audiovisual services from the basement to the main entrance. The quickness of that transition coupled is a strong testament to both the unrivaled popularity of video collections as well as to the unlimited potential a well developed and managed video collection holds for meeting patron needs.

1

THE VIDEO COLLECTION

In our zeal to have video accepted as a mainstream service in libraries, it is tempting to say that developing a video collection is just like developing a book collection. In a sense this is true, yet there are some special considerations about video. One of these is in the area of selection and acquisitions.

COLLECTION BREADTH AND BALANCE

As with any library collection, a good video collection is the direct result of solid collection planning and development. It is not simply a matter of choosing "hot" movie titles that duplicate the corner video store. In the next chapter we will examine collection development policies for video in detail. The following chapters will discuss the art of locating, evaluating, and purchasing a really good library video collection. First, however, for video, as with any library collection, there are certain basic decisions to be made about breadth and balance. A starting place is in establishing the target audience for the collection. In the case of public libraries, both the library's mission statement and community demographics are considerations. For school and academic libraries, the age level of students and curricular goals of the institution will be the central guides. The public library's mission statement can be a very important guidepost. A public library that is fulfilling a recreational reading need will perhaps most appropriately concentrate on popular feature films, classics, and how-to tapes; while one concentrating on research will want to spend more on documentary and educational tapes.

These are important decisions, in that there are so many videotapes available on the market (more than 140,000)[2], and library budgets being what they are, very few libraries are able to purchase everything that appears interesting. So how do you decide what types of videos to purchase?

FICTION VS. NONFICTION

In this discussion we will use the very book-like terms "fiction" and "nonfiction" to divide generally the video collection into feature films (fiction), and documentaries, educational programs, and how-tos (nonfiction). Schools and academic libraries will consider all titles nonfiction, as certain feature films are used in classes. For example, film adaptations of Shakespeare (Olivier and/or Branagh's *Henry V*) are commonly used, as are films on sociological subjects (*Rain Man*) and history (*Schindler's List*).

A Dozen Documentaries

A highly personal list that only hints at the wealth of wonderful material available from independent producers and distributors.

The Children of Theatre Street
Fascinating look inside the famous Kirov Ballet School in its Soviet heyday. 1977, Kultur Video.

Complaints of a Dutiful Daughter
Wrenching, but ultimately life-affirming, portrait of a family's struggle with Alzheimer's Disease. 1995, Women Make Movies.

Ethnic Notions
Marlin Riggs' landmark work on the depiction of African-Americans in the media. 1987, California Newsreel.

FDR
A monumentally skillful portrait of Franklin Roosevelt. 1995, PBS.

Garlic Is As Good As Ten Mothers
Everything you wanted to know, and more, about the "stinking rose." A film by Les Blank. 1980, Flower Films.

Georgia O'Keeffe
Fine film portrait of the gritty and legendary artist. 1986, Home Vision.

The Good Fight
Reminiscences of the colorful men and women of the Abraham Lincoln Brigade. 1984, Kino on Video.

He Makes Me Feel Like Dancin'
Jacques d'Amboise, New York City Ballet legend, teaches New York City schoolchildren (and even city policemen) the joy of dancing. 1984, Direct Cinema.

The Man Who Planted Trees
Though not a documentary, this needs to be in every library. A beautiful, animated work for all ages, it is the inspiring story of a Basque shepherd who literally changed the world around him. 1987, Direct Cinema.

Marshall, Texas; Marshall, Texas
From Bill Moyers' "A Walk through the Twentieth Century," this portrait of a town that produced both Moyers and Civil Rights leader, James Farmer, is the epitome of erudite television. 1982, PBS.

Say Amen, Somebody
An uplifting, joyful look at gospel music and the people who give it life. 1980, PBS.

Shoah
An enormous achievement, this nine-and-a-half hour epic tells the story of the Holocaust through interviews with survivors, former Nazis, and German civilians, as well as archival footage. 1985, Paramount.

For most public libraries, the decision regarding the balance between fiction and nonfiction is one of the most important. Some libraries have decided only to purchase nonfiction videos, feeling that the local video stores fulfill the demand for popular titles. A strong reason to adopt this policy is that it is true that the public library is the only resource in most communities for anything but the most mainstream popular titles. Even the largest video stores give minimal shelf space to the "special interest" categories, and these are largely dominated by World War II documentaries and exercise tapes. Other public libraries adopt the "give them what they want" philosophy; collecting primarily the mainstream feature films available in video stores. This is certainly a popular choice with much of the public, much like concentrating on a book collection consisting primarily of bestsellers. If the library's role is chiefly recreational, this is an appropriate choice. Most libraries, however, choose to balance somewhere in the middle. In recent years, the choice most often was a 60 percent-40 percent balance, with non-fiction most often being given the largest share of the budget.

Fiction

With fiction, it would seem simply a matter of choosing a wholesale vendor and ordering familiar titles; yet decisions need to be made here, too. Every year there are a few hundred feature films released in the United States, and only a handful that become mainstream hits. As with novels, those receiving the most press are not necessarily the best. There is a real opportunity for the library to bring "small" but excellent films to an appreciative audience that wasn't found at the local mall's cineplex. In addition to popular American features, the library will want to consider film classics, foreign titles, and limited release features.

A few years ago I was in a meeting that included representatives of the video store business. I was both stunned and pleased to hear a very sophisticated video businessman state that he felt the public library was really the hope for the history of film, because video stores will continue to stock only the most popular titles, while the library will continue to stock the full range of titles. While video-on-demand will certainly change this to some degree, it is still a real possibility that the library video collection will become the archive of "movies."

In building an excellent feature film collection, there are some natural guidelines. One is genre. The library will want to have a good representation of dramas, comedies, westerns, musicals, detective stories, and action adventure. For a representative collection there will also need to be a span of time represented. For example, in the area of musicals, it would be important to include some Busby Berkeley "all singing, all dancing" extravaganzas from the Thirties, some Astaire and Rogers, a group of titles from the golden age of MGM, such as *Singin' in the Rain, Bandwagon*, and *The Wizard of Oz*, as well as the film versions of Broadway musicals like *Oklahoma, Sound of Music*, and *Hello Dolly*. Additionally, the collection should have some of the darker and/or smaller musicals of the 70s and 80s, like *All That Jazz, Pennies From Heaven, Footloose*, and *Dirty Dancing*.

In addition to genres, the collection librarian will want to have representation of certain film artists. In moviemaking, the director is as important to the work as the author is to a book. But film has additional important artists as well, such as screenwriters, cinematographers, and, of course, actors. This wide range of contributors to one work can, of course, cause catalogers to run for aspirin, and libraries must make decisions about what to include in the catalog. But in building a collection, it is very important to have a good representation of serious and popular artists. The good collection will need to include film artists from various eras, with an emphasis on directors and actors for the popular collection, and inclusion of screenwriters and cinematographers in more serious collections. For example, works by directors Cecil B. DeMille, Alfred Hitchcock, John Ford, Vincente Minnelli, Ida Lupino, Frank Capra, Martin Scorsese, George Lucas, and Spike Lee (just to name a few) represent the history and development of American film.

So far I have focused entirely on American film and film artists. However, collections will also want to include foreign works, both in subtitled and original language versions. While Hollywood has dominated the mainstream "movie" market worldwide from the very beginning of the film industry, it is by no means the only, or even the most interesting, film community in the world. In point of fact, India's film industry is larger, and several in Europe produce higher-quality films. In recent years, the opening of communications has brought fascinating work to this country from China and Eastern Europe. Several African nations are releasing beautiful works on the international market, as are a number in Latin America. It is in the area of foreign films that the public library, in particular, can make a vital contribution. Video stores tend to stock only the most recent, or most classic, of foreign films. As with the rest of commercial video store fare, these works tend to be limited to those that played in local art theaters.

In purchasing foreign films for the library collection, there is at least one hard and fast rule: Subtitles are *almost always* preferable to dubbing. While it is more work to read titles off the screen, particularly off a television screen, in recent years great strides have been made in making the subtitles more readable. Dubbing, even when done well, detracts from performances, and nearly always comes off sounding stiff and flat. Depending on the library's constituency, the collection might also include some films in languages other than English without subtitles. Only a small number of productions are ever released in English. The greatest challenge in this area is in locating titles for purchase. One excellent source for foreign features, as well as alternative materials, is Facets Multimedia, 1517 West Fullerton Avenue, Chicago, IL 60614 (1-800-331-6197). Additionally, more than one resourceful librarian has reported that excellent sources for purchasing foreign language films are ethnic grocery and variety stores. Depending on the size of your town or city, this may or may not be a useful suggestion.

Nonfiction

Probably the most logical method for choosing nonfiction videos is to follow the pattern of the library's cataloging system—Dewey or Library of Congress (LC). This certainly works well for keeping the collection balanced and in line with the library's mission, but there are some special considerations about video that should be taken into account. While it is true that there is now a video on every subject known to humankind, not all video subjects should be considered equally. Personally, I felt that critical mass had been reached and surpassed with the announcement a few years ago of the video on garage sales, featuring Phyllis Diller. A good title for a popular library collection, nonetheless.

Using the Dewey Decimal System as a guide, it is clear that some subjects are not only appropriately treated on video, but in some cases are a better choice for the transmission of information. For example, in the 900 range, Twentieth Century historical events have all been recorded on film. A good video collection with any research charge will need to have a heavy representation in this area. For example, while we are deprived of a moving picture record of Abraham Lincoln delivering the Gettysburg address, we do have the opportunity to actually see and hear Martin Luther King's landmark "I Have a Dream" speech. Two world wars, the first moon landing, the assassination and funeral of John F. Kennedy, and the coronation of Elizabeth II all are recorded in detail. So many changes have not only been recorded by, but affected by, the motion picture camera. The Vietnam War as broadcast daily on television brought cataclysmic change to American society. More recently moving pictures of Somali and Ethiopian

Who Says There's Nothing Good on Television?

Below are some excellent miniseries/series highlights/individual programs originally produced for television. I have left off the obvious (e.g., I, Claudius, Upstairs, Downstairs, and Jewel in the Crown). These should be available from major commercial distributors.

And the Band Played On
Star-studded, but still moving film based on Randy Shilts' landmark book on the AIDS epidemic. 140 minutes, HBO. 1993.

Anne of Green Gables
A stunningly wonderful adaptation of the Lucy Maud Montgomery books. Two cassettes. Buena Vista. 1985.

Danger UXB
Unlikely as it sounds, this story of the Royal Engineers bomb squad during World War II is absolutely riveting. Five cassettes, Signals. 1981.

The Flame Trees of Thika
Based on the memoirs of Elspeth Huxley, this is a beautifully-produced series about an English family on an East Africa coffee plantation in the early years of the century. Four cassettes, Signals. 1981.

Gypsy
The musical may have been written for Ethel Merman, but Bette Midler was born to play it in this TV production. 150 minutes, Cabin Fever. 1993.

The Hitchhiker's Guide to the Galaxy
The ultimate in cult sci-fi spoofs. Six episodes from the BBC series, CBS/Fox. 1981.

The House of Eliott
For those who could never get enough of *Upstairs, Downstairs*, the same team wrote and produced this series about two sisters starting their own fashion house in 1920s London. Six cassettes, Arts & Entertainment. 1992.

A Perfect Spy
Vintage John LeCarre, produced by the BBC. Three cassettes, CBS/Fox. 1988.

The Positively True Adventures of the Alleged Texas Cheerleader-Murdering Mom
The title says it all, (except what a deliciously droll film this is) with a standout performance by Holly Hunter. Ninety-nine minutes, HBO. 1993.

The Summer of My German Soldier
A quietly moving adaptation of Bette Green's novel in which a young American girl befriends a German POW during World War II. Ninety-nine minutes, MTI. 1978.

A Town Like Alice
The romantic saga of a British woman and an Australian soldier who are both POWs of the Japanese in World War II Malaysia. Based on the Nevil Shute novel. Two cassettes, New World. 1985.

Who Am I This Time?
Based on a Vonnegut story, this warm and funny PBS production features Susan Sarandon and Christopher Walken as two shy people who only can express themselves by acting in their community theater. Sixty minutes, Monterey Home Video. 1982.

famine have caused a demand for action from around the world, as have the gut-wrenching pictures of the devastation in Sarajevo.

Also in the 900 scheme is the huge area of geography and travel. This area ranges from video guidebooks from well-known travel publishers, to educational geography programs, and personal travel memoirs. "Armchair" travel has long been an immensely popular segment of public library audiovisual collections.

There is also a wide range of appropriate choices in the area of the 300s—social documentaries are a mainstay of independent filmmaking, and an example of a type of material that is often only available to the public through one-time public television broadcast (if the filmmaker is lucky), and then in the library.

Good material is also available in the 500s and 600s—health and fitness. In addition to the ubiquitous exercise tapes, there is a wide choice on health care, nutrition, childrearing, etc. And in the scientific area, there are countless excellent programs on all phases of science and nature.

Another popular field for popular collections is the "how-tos," many which fall into the 600s and 700s—home repair, cooking, sewing, hobbies and crafts, and sports. This is another part of the collection that calls for serious video collecting. In many cases, videos in these areas better fulfill an informational purpose than do books on the same subject. Whether it is how to wallpaper a corner, prepare a complex dessert, or successfully bunt a baseball, a moving picture is superior to reading. And the option of repeating instructions over and over is as close as the freeze-frame and rewind buttons on the VCR.

In the arts sections of the 700s and 800s, there is also a wide range of materials available on video. Recorded performances of operas, ballets, orchestral concerts, and plays are all important in the video collection. Here is an opportunity to offer a range of interpretations of the same work featuring different artists, and to offer the delight of concert hall and theater performance to all but the few who have the option to experience them live. How many of us will ever have the opportunity to see Placido Domingo at La Scala? Or had the chance to witness Nureyev, Barishnikov, or Fonteyn performing in their prime at Lincoln Center? Video gives us those experiences.

At the same time, there are subjects that do not as readily lend themselves to the video format. While there are excellent programs in the areas of religion, philosophy, and literature, for example, much of the material and information in those fields are more appropriately presented in print or on audiocassette. There are some wonderful exceptions, however, such as Bill Moyers' interviews with Joseph Campbell, and the superb *Voices and Visions* series on modern American poetry.

A Dewey Chart of Selected Video Subjects

000 *General Works*
Computer Instruction—general and specific programs

100 *Psychology*
Personal Motivation
Popular Psychology

200 *Religion*
Bible Study: dramatization of Bible stories
Series on major world religions
Documentaries on sects and cults

300 *Social Science*
Social documentaries
multicultural subjects
aging
physically and mentally challenged
world issues
current events
Drug and Alcohol Addiction
Vocational guidance
job interviewing
career videos
SAT, ACT preparation

400 *Language*
Foreign language study
English language study
American Sign Language study
Basic reading and writing skills for adults

500 *Science*
Nature documentaries
Environmental concerns
Physical and earth science documentaries

600 *Applied Science*
Health issues
Smoking cessation
Diet and nutrition
Fitness and exercise
Childbirth and parenting skills
Sex education
Business management (see also 300)
Space exploration
Cooking

A Dewey Chart of Selected Video Subjects (cont.)

House and garden
Hobbies (see also 700)

700 *The Arts*
Museum documentaries
Biographies of artists and performers
Architecture
Opera performances
Dance performances
Dance instruction
Classical music performances
Popular music performances
Musical performances with added visuals
Musical instrument instruction
Film and television documentaries
Cinema history
Classic television shows
Crafts instruction (see also 600)
Sports documentaries
Sports skills instruction
Photography

800 *Literature*
Short story adaptations
Profiles of writers
Performances of plays
Public speaking instruction

900 *History and Travel*
Political history documentaries
Military history documentaries
Geographical documentaries
Biographies of political leaders
Biographies of historical figures
Armchair travel
Video travel guides

Ten Sleepers

A highly personal list of titles to enhance your feature film collection. The films should be available through any major video supplier.

Breaking Away
Exciting bicycle racing; coming of age comedy-drama; and "townies" vs. students—what more could you ask for? Directed by Peter Yates, Academy Award screenplay by Steve Tesich, 1979.

The Commitments
A quirky, touching story about a group of Irish kids who want to bring soul music to Dublin. Directed by Alan Parker, 1991.

Crossing Delancey
A charming feel-good tale of a modern urban woman learning about what really counts in life. Directed by Joan Micklin Silver, 1988.

El Norte
The gripping tale of a Guatemalan brother and sister escaping to the United States, and then struggling in their new homeland. In Spanish and English, with English subtitles. Directed by Gregory Nava, 1983.

Local Hero
What happens when a Texas multinational oil company decides to purchase a Scottish town for its mineral rights (from a Scottish perspective)? Directed by Bill Forsyth, 1983.

Nothing But a Man
A landmark film about African-American life in the South during the 1960s, remarkable for its well-rounded characters and compelling view of racism. Directed by Michael Roemer, 1964.

Sounder
Highly-regarded at its release, this tale of African-American sharecroppers in the Depression is still a superb family film. Directed by Martin Ritt, 1972.

That Man from Rio
Thoroughly entertaining adventure that is also the world's longest shaggy dog story. Starring Jean-Paul Belmondo. French with English subtitles. Directed by Phillipe de Broca, 1964.

A Thousand Clowns
Brilliant screenplay (Herb Gardner from his own play) and performances by Jason Robards, Martin Balsam, and Barbara Harris make this a great film about a lovable nonconformist fighting the system. Directed by Fred Coe, 1965.

Whistle Down the Wind
A lovely allegory about some English children who think a criminal on the lam in their barn is Jesus. Directed by Bryan Forbes, 1962.

It is also important to remember another major contribution made by video programs, that of offering valuable information and insights to those unable to read, or those who prefer the visual format. There have been countless studies by educational academicians that show beyond question that people learn in different ways. In other words, some learn best from the printed page, others by hearing, and still others by watching. The best of all learning circumstances offer all three. This is true whether the learning environment is the classroom or the living room. It is therefore important for libraries to make information available in all formats. Technology has given us a tremendous opportunity by making it possible to fulfill the needs of all types of learners.

At the same time, video programs are a tremendous boon to those who are not able to read, or unable to read at a level sufficient for processing complex information. Video can provide essential assistance for the non-reader. Information about how to apply for a job, how to prepare nutritious meals, and how to repair a car can be of enormous importance. There are also excellent literacy programs available on video.

In many cases, the barrier to print is not literacy *per se*, but literacy in English. In addition to programs on how to speak English, it is important to offer programs in foreign languages commonly spoken in the library's service area. Again, these come in both fiction and nonfiction. In the section on acquisitions in Chapter 3, I will discuss sources for videos in languages other than English.

CHILDREN'S VIDEOS

In a number of surveys which were conducted in the late 1980s and early 1990s about video collections in libraries, almost all public librarians listed children's materials at the top of the list as far as popularity and priority for purchase. The availability of children's video has grown like wildfire over the past ten years. That is both good and bad news. There's a lot to choose from, certainly, but a vast majority is very bad, or mediocre.

An important collection development decision is what percentage of the library's collection should be devoted to children's videos. In this case, a good guide might be the library's book collection. Presumably this balance reflects the constituency the library serves. If the library is in a neighborhood with many families, this number will probably be greater than in an inner-city branch serving mostly a business community.

With children's videos it is even more important than with adult videos to look beyond the local video store for guidance for selection. While most parents declare a strong interest in providing

Ten Foreign Language Classics

Some excellent titles for a library collection, going beyond the obvious Fellini, Bergman, etc.

Allegro Non Troppo
Known as the Italian "Fantasia," and set to Ravel's *Bolero*, the highlight of this animated family classic is the story of evolution. Directed by Bruno Bozzetto, 1976.

Bagdad Cafe
Very quirky tale of a German woman abandoned at a Mojave Desert motel by her wayward husband. Though it is in English, it is from a German perspective. Directed by Percy Adlon, 1988.

Black Orpheus
Wonderful music and beautiful atmosphere add to this re-telling of the legend of Orpheus and Eurydice. Set in the black neighborhoods of Rio de Janeiro during Carnaval. Portuguese with English subtitles. Directed by Marcel Camus, 1958.

Les Mistons
Very early and charming Truffaut film about adolescent boys stalking and worshipping an older girl. Directed by François Truffaut, 1957.

Moscow Does Not Believe in Tears
Set in 1950s Russia, three female factory workers face life in much the same way any three women anywhere might. It was a revelation in the days of the Cold War. Directed by Vladimir Menshov, 1980.

My Father's Glory (and also My Mother's Castle)
Two wonderfully evocative tales of childhood-based on the stories of Marcel Pagnol. French. Directed by Yves Robert, 1991.

The Night of the Shooting Stars
Moving, poignant story of a small Italian village torn between the opposing forces of World War II. Directed by Paolo and Vittorio Taviani, 1982.

Raise the Red Lantern
Gorgeous to look at, this is a fascinating tale of the 1920s role of women in Chinese society. Directed by Zhang Yimou, 1991.

Rashomon
The oft-copied, but never-equaled tale of four viewpoints of the same crime in medieval Japan. Directed by Akira Kurosawa, 1951.

War and Peace
The remarkable six-and-a-half-hour Russian adaptation of the Tolstoy novel. Beautiful, exhaustive (and exhausting), no other historical epic is quite like it. Directed by Sergei Bondarchuk, 1968.

quality for their offspring, very few are versed in any programming beyond Disney features, programs based on the latest toys, and some recycled TV fare. Not all of this programming is bad, by any means, but there is really a wealth of good-to-excellent quality material available that doesn't get the publicity of programming exposed through the mainstream media.

As with adult materials, there are certain producers and distributors of video programming specializing in quality children's programming. Some of these are holdovers from the heyday of educational 16mm films, when there was a great deal of original programming being produced for classroom use. While this industry has been greatly reduced, there are still some educational programs being offered for specific age groups on a variety of subjects.

Some of the best children's videos are based on children's literature. Certain producers are noted for quality book adaptations. Weston Woods (sold as Children's Circle on the consumer market) is probably the best-known of this group. I feel some hesitation in discussing video programs in this way, because while it is true that viewing book-based programs can encourage reading, a video should not be judged on this basis. Just because it is book-based does not mean it is a good piece of filmmaking. Conversely, there are versions of books that are better on film. Or, a certain video version of a book or story may shed new light on a work of literature. One example that comes to mind is Michael Sporn's animated version of Hans Christian Andersen's *The Red Shoes*. This fully animated version of the classic tale is set in modern Harlem, with the modern urban setting adding immeasurably to the tale and its moral.

Any look at children's video collections would be incomplete without a discussion of animation. It is certainly a fact that animated films are immensely popular with children. Unfortunately, a couple of generations of Saturday morning TV fare has given a bad name to and a skewed vision of animation. What is seen in most of these programs can only be described as "quick and dirty." The producers use what is known as "limited" animation in these shows. The characters are stiff, drawn unimaginatively, and move only every few frames, so there is no flow to the action.

Quality animation, on the other hand, is a true art form. Good animators have recognizable styles, using movement, color, and detail to enhance the story. The above-mentioned Michael Sporn, Churchill Media's John Matthews (a master of puppet animation), the works of producer Joshua Greene's "Stories to Remember," and, almost invariably, the picture book-based works from Weston Woods, are examples of animation excellence. While some of these artists are represented in video store collections, most are not.

Ten Children's Classics (and Soon-To-Be Classics)

These are titles not commonly available in video stores. When possible, the distributor holding the public performance rights is listed—these are all good for library programs. (Addresses for these distributors are in the single-source distributor list on pages 43 and 44 in this book.) Or, get in touch with Weston Woods. This superb production company has released many book adaptations under its own name and, in the home video market, as Children's Circle. You cannot go wrong in selecting any title from their catalog.

Bizet's Dream
Set in Paris in 1875, this lovely film features Michelle, who finds it difficult to understand her piano teacher, distracted by the writing of his opera, "Carmen." From the same series as *Beethoven Lives Upstairs*. Ages 8-12. Sony. 1995.

A Boy, A Dog and A Frog
Live-action adaptation of the Mercer Mayer book. A charming child actor and a masterful frog actor. Ages 3-8. Phoenix/BFA (public performance). 1981.

Harry Comes Home (also *Harry and the Lady Next Door*)
Hilarious adaptation of the *Harry, the Dirty Dog* book. Live action, featuring the enchanting Jake, dog actor extraordinaire. Ages 6-12. Barr Films (public performance). 1991.

Make a Wish, Molly
A sequel to the classic *Molly's Pilgrim*, in which Molly faces problems in school regarding her religious beliefs. Both *Make a Wish, Molly* and *Molly's Pilgrim* should be in library collections. Ages 7-10. Phoenix Learning Group (Phoenix/BFA) (public performance). 1995.

The Mouse and the Motorcycle (also *Runaway Ralph* and *Ralph S. Mouse*)
These mixtures of animation and live action are wonderful adaptations of the Beverly Cleary favorites. Animation by John Matthews. Ages 6-12. Churchill Media (public performance). 1988.

The Red Balloon
This classic never goes out of style. A lovely, lyrical story of a young Parisian boy and his magical balloon friend. Ages 6 and up. Distributed by Columbia/TriStar. 1956.

Red Shoes
A contemporary re-telling of the Andersen fairy tale, set in Harlem and featuring the animation of Michael Sporn. Ages 8-12. Lucerne Media (public performance). 1990.

Sadako and the 1000 Paper Cranes
Beautiful animation and gentle narration by Liv Ullman tell the story of Sadako, a victim of radiation sickness after the atomic bomb is dropped on Hiroshima. Ages 8-12. Informed Democracy, P.O. Box 67, Santa Cruz, CA 95063 (public performance). 1991.

Whitewash
In this animated story, based on a true incident, a small African-American girl is cornered by a racist gang and has white shoe polish sprayed on her face. The love and support she receives in the terrible aftermath is a gentle, but strong, antidote to hate. Ages 8-12. Churchill Media (public performance). 1994.

You Don't Have To Die
Based on his own book, Jason movingly tells children of his successful fight with cancer. Live action with animation. Ages 6-adult. Ambrose Video (public performance). 1988.

As the video industry has matured, more attention has been paid to all types of children's programming, including nonfiction. More and more programs are being released to the home market in the fields of nature, science, ecology, community awareness, and personal growth, as well as a myriad of how-tos in the fields of sports and arts and crafts. These programs really aren't hard to find, and are priced affordably. I continue to be mystified, then, as to why these "family-oriented" chains seem so careless in their selection of titles. Developing a quality children's video collection is a real opportunity for a public library to provide a service not readily available elsewhere in the community.

POPULAR AND INFORMATIONAL VIDEOS

As we discussed earlier in this chapter, an important decision that needs to be made in building a quality video collection concerns the balance between mainstream entertainment videos and informational titles. It is also true that within the nonfiction collection, decisions need to be made concerning the balance between mainstream and more specialized programs.

This balance question is one that isn't exclusive to the audiovisual collection, nor is it new with video. The vast majority of people who use the library have a better idea of the breadth of print material available than they do of the breadth of visual material available. This is a big part of the perception that some in the community may have that video is a "frill." When "video" is mentioned it is most likely to evoke Hollywood mainstream movies in people's minds, while most are aware that the book collection has room for both Stephen King and Stephen Crane.

I will admit to leaning towards emphasizing videos in the collection that are not so readily available elsewhere. This is, of course, a decision for each library to make in the context of its constituency. In most communities inexpensive rental of popular titles is readily available. No matter how many copies of the latest action/adventure title the library purchases, the immediate demand can't be met in any case. While making sure that community demand for popular titles is appropriately addressed in planning the collection, it seems to me that the lion's share of the budget might better be spent on a variety of titles not available in the video store.

While serious social documentaries are certainly included in this group (more follows in the next section), the informational titles really cover a vast territory in both seriousness and challenge. As mentioned above, video can play an important role in assisting people with life skills. This can mean information on prenatal care, child rearing, and job interview skills. It can mean clear information on health management from quitting smoking to diabetes. Or it can be as frivolous as choosing makeup or planning a fantasy vacation. The fact of the matter is, most people can't afford to buy a video on every subject that interests them, or to purchase all the titles available on their favorite pastime or hobby.

Another important community consideration is materials for both the hearing and the visually impaired. Many videos, particularly in the educational category, are available with closed captioning for the hearing impaired. Librarians will want to seek these out, and to also clearly label them on each video box. More and more titles are available with a descriptive track for the visually impaired. One good example is *A Taste for Death*, the latest P.D. James novel adapted for television and broadcast on PBS. A version is available in which descriptions of action are included by a narrator between dialogue, so that a visually impaired individual can enjoy the production. The source for these programs is Descriptive Video Service, WGBH Educational Foundation, 12 Western Avenue, Boston, MA 02134.

While most of this section has been addressed specifically to the public library, schools and academic librarians will also want to consider titles outside the strict classroom instructional vein. "Homework" and/or recreational collections in school/academic libraries are increasingly popular.

THE INDEPENDENT VIEW

When the video revolution took place in the mid-1980s, filmmakers and film librarians alike were convinced that the day of the independent film had finally arrived. Everyone believed that low-cost video would open up a vast market for the specialized and the alternative. For a number of reasons, some of them still enigmatic, this hasn't happened. A creative and struggling filmmaking community is still struggling to survive financially while remaining creative. "Independents" here are defined as film works created outside the confines of Hollywood and network television. Very often they reflect a highly personal style and point-of-view. Most documentaries fall into this category—much of what is broadcast on PBS, Arts & Entertainment, Bravo, and the Discovery Channel, for example.

Because the audience for these works has never been (and it appears never will be) in the millions, and distribution is often through a single source, the price of these programs tends to be higher. This puts the librarian in a real bind. While few libraries can boast a budget large enough to purchase anything interesting that comes along the pike, the overwhelming demand is for the inexpensive and popular mainstream titles the public or the classroom teacher knows about. It is tempting just to go along and spend the budget on easily affordable and popular videos. This, however, eliminates a vast amount of creative, interesting, multidimensional work. It is my strong recommendation that even the library with the most popular charge assign at least some of the materials budget to purchase the specialized, the quirky, and the creative. Our collections, our patrons, and future generations will all lose if this vital form of expression dies because of lack of financial support.

SPECIAL COLLECTIONS

As video collections in libraries mature, interesting opportunities develop for offering unique and special services. Because there is so much excellent material available, much of it never seen in the mainstream video business, special collections can make a real contribution to various user constituencies.

Sharing resources has long been a tradition with book collections, whether it is in the area of straightforward interlibrary loan, or the building of in-depth subject collections through cooperative collection development. For example, one library in a community with a great interest in the arts might want to allocate more resources to build a really comprehensive video collection of opera, ballet, and concert performances. There are currently, for example, five different productions of *Turandot* available on video, featuring a variety of singers, companies, and productions. Another library might choose to specialize in the cinema from a country with a large representation in the community. This collection would probably include both original language and subtitled versions of films, and examples of documentary, arts, and other offerings. Another innovative cooperative approach might be for public, school, and academic libraries in a geographic area to work together and share collections of local interest.

The library can also serve an archival function for a constituency. This might take the form of organizing and storing tapes of city council meetings, school functions, or local events. With the widespread use of camcorders and local access cable, a great deal of material is now stored on tape, but organized access and knowledgeable selection of what to keep is a service that librarians are uniquely qualified to perform.

Another special collection a library might consider is local history. More than simply the recording of city council and high school athletic events, an oral history project can now evolve into video history. The library might want to consider the videotaping of interviews with local pioneers, former city officials, or artists and writers who are long-time residents, or were born and raised locally. In addition to reminiscences, video affords the opportunity to "go on location" to discuss the history of a community, viewing buildings and other local landmarks with those who have lived in a location for a long time. It also offers the opportunity to show works of art, crafts, and demonstrate musical performance. An example, though not typical of most communities, is the visual history project at the Schomberg Center for Black History and Culture of the New York Public Library. Media librarian James Murray tells of the wonderful opportunity he had to record modern dance pioneer, Katherine Dunham, demonstrating and teaching her art to dancers from the Alvin Ailey Dance Theater. While most communities won't have a Katherine Dunham, every town has its own creative members, as well as those whose memories will provide an important documentation of local history.

BIBLIOGRAPHY

Barnow, Erik. *Documentary: A History of the Non-Fiction Film* (Rev. ed.). New York, Oxford, 1983.

Boyle, Deirdre. *Video Classics: A Guide to Video Art and Documentary Tapes*. Phoenix, AZ, Oryx Press, 1986.

Brown, Lucy Gregor. *Core Media Collection for Elementary Schools*. New York, R.R. Bowker.

———. *Core Media Collection for Secondary Schools*. New York, R.R. Bowker.

Franco, Debra. *Alternative Visions: Distributing Independent Media in a Home Video World*. Los Angeles, American Film Institute, 1990.

Green, Diana Huss, ed. *Parents Choice Guide to Videocassettes for Children*. Mt. Vernon, NY, Consumers Union.

Mason, Sally. "A Declaration for Independents." *Wilson Library Bulletin*, December, 1991, pp. 68–9.

——— and James Scholtz, eds. *Video For Libraries: Special Interest Video for Small and Medium-Sized Public Libraries*, Chicago, ALA, 1988.

Northern, Penny. "Video's Visual Heritage." *Booklist*, 84:21, July, 1988, pp. 1853–6.

Pitman, Randy and Elliott Swanson. *Video Movies: A Core Collection for Libraries*. Santa Barbara, CA, ABC-Clio, 1990.

The Elementary School Library Collection. Greensboro, NC, Bro-Dart Foundation. Latest edition.

2 EVALUATING VIDEO TITLES

It's a funny thing about motion media. Virtually all of us have literally thousands of hours of experience in viewing and analyzing motion pictures, whether we are conscious we are doing it or not. Every time we discuss a current movie with a friend, shake our heads over the inanity of the latest sit-com, or talk with family members about the ethics of tabloid television journalism, we are practicing media criticism. Given that all of the discussion about the damage watching violent or low-quality productions may be doing to the younger generations, it is ironic that mainstream educators at all levels—including library schools—still resolutely refuse to offer tools for intelligent criticism. Nonetheless, two things are apparent. One, with the continuing growth of motion media as entertainment and information deliverers, it is essential to develop skills in evaluating what is seen; and two, we all know a great deal more about media criticism than we think we do. In this chapter, I will discuss the elements of a good video, and the special aspects that are important in evaluating videos for library selection.

Evaluating visual material is different than books in some essential ways. For one thing, evaluating a book is a one-dimensional experience. While typeface, binding and illustrations are important, the evaluation is based largely on the communication of the words on the page; in a video, presentation, words, sound, and pictures are equally important. This is why, especially at first, an evaluator may need to view a single program more than once. No, it is not necessary to become Pauline Kael or Roger Ebert. Most librarians today, even with the most noble intentions, do not have the time to thoroughly evaluate every potential title for the collection. But it is essential that some experience be gained in evaluation so that selectors can make intelligent choices.

I often joke (only half-kiddingly) that after more than twenty-five years of viewing and evaluating motion pictures for libraries, I have developed the foolproof three-level evaluation:

- I fall asleep or make a grocery list in my head: This one is a loser.
- I am attentive all the way through: A good video.
- The hair on my arms stands on end: This one is special.

In a more serious vein, there are three main elements in evaluating a video program for a library collection.

- Content
- Technical Aspects
- Usage

Within each of these three elements there is a lot to analyze. The following sections give a practical guide for busy librarians who have more dedication than time.

CONTENT

Content of a video is evaluated similarly to a book. Such considerations as the presentation of the information, the overall organization of the material, and the quality of the writing of the script are included.

PRESENTATION OF INFORMATION

In any video production in the non-fiction category, the first consideration has to be the information presented. In this case, videos are just like books. No matter how creative or beautiful the technical aspects of a video may be, a video is worthless if the information is inaccurate or misleading. Again, as with books, checking accuracy may be done in a number of ways. The authority of the producers may be a clue, reading reviews in professional journals is essential, and consulting with others on the library's staff or in the community can be of great assistance. Obviously, not every video can or needs to be carefully vetted, but with some titles, particularly those in the area of health care, the library really has an obligation to be sure the material is accurate. Accuracy, however, is not the same as objectivity. To be good, a video does not necessarily need to be even-handed in its viewpoint. In fact, the very best of documentary filmmaking is very like the best in the "letters to the editor" of a newspaper. Point-of-view is essential to the work. It has sometimes been the practice, however, to eliminate from library collections videos that we term "biased."

Yet, these "biased" films are often eloquent and artistically riveting—fine examples of persuasive arguments for strongly held beliefs. Without question the medium of "film" is a strong persuader. Seeing and hearing at the same time can have great emotional impact. For example, the plight of the starving and suffering Somali people led to direct U.S. involvement there because we were all witnesses thanks to our televisions. There is little doubt that newspaper editorials, no matter how impassioned, would ever have evoked the same response. These are important documents for a library to make available to its constituency.

It is ironic, then, that the very thing a good filmmaker can do best can lead to uninformed criticism of the work. Filmmakers are sometimes taken to task for not being "objective." Point-of-view is an important tool for an artist. Alternative viewpoints, whether for gay rights or the right to life, can make viewers very uncomfortable. Good filmmaking shouldn't be punished because it does its job well. This is another reason for careful evaluation of video materials. Recognizing good work and making it available to the library's constituency is vital to a really quality collection.

ORGANIZATION

Here, again, is an area where video is very much like print material. It doesn't matter how essential the information is if it isn't presented in an understandable fashion. The program should have some logical order to it, and points need to be made clearly and completely. Any conclusion should be spelled out, and the expertise of those delivering the information should be established.

Beyond the actual delivery of the information is the question of whether the presentation is a good use of the medium. While there are videos on every subject these days, every subject does not necessarily lend itself to becoming a good video. "Talking heads" have long been a foundation of informational film and video productions. They can be extremely useful, particularly if mixed with moving images and other visual material. Filmed lectures or discussions need to be of a subject of incredibly high interest to justify the use of the medium. There are notable examples, I must admit. The superb *Ethics in America* series, in which prominent Americans struggled with thorny ethical questions while we all got to watch, was riveting television, and later riveting video viewing; but this series is definitely an exception.

Another important criteria is whether the use of moving images enhanced the presentation of the information. It is also important to consider the value of the information being presented to those in the library's constituency for whom reading about the subject is difficult or impossible.

SCRIPT

This element of video content applies to all video, whether non-fiction or fiction, or even videos without dialogue or narration. All of us who watch films have first-hand experience with both good and bad screenplays. We are pleased by the unexpected and the original in story and dialogue. We cringe at unbelievable situations and clichés of speech and action, though they are sometimes good for a laugh. Eloquence is not limited to the printed page, though really good scripts are not all that common. An example of consistent eloquence in non-fiction film and video writing are the programs from Bill Moyers. He and his staff consistently find ways to make the most static and mundane subjects lively, and even, sometimes, profound. This is done through a masterly combination of words and images.

"Script" is not as evident in the style of documentary we are most used to—the combination of interviews, film footage, and voice-over narration. Selecting the right questions to ask in filmed interviews and evoking interesting responses, though, as well as selecting and editing them into a film with the appropriate images, is high art.

APPROPRIATENESS

Because of both the wide range of materials available on the video market today and the limits of most library budgets, "appropriateness" can be the deciding factor for many video titles. Once again, this relates directly to the mission of the library, and the balance of the collection.

For school and academic libraries, appropriateness is key. This would include determining if the video in question in some way supports the institution's curriculum and if its content is age-appropriate. For school libraries, selection by age and subject is fundamental. But within those age groups and subject areas, there is always a wide range of quality available, so that evaluating remains important beyond, say, finding a fourth-grade geography program.

In public libraries, appropriateness can also be broken down by age categories. Most public libraries, for example, establish a collection for children, whether it is located in the video department or in the children's department. There is also the consideration of videos specifically of interest to young adults, as well as those of interest to businesspeople, travelers, and arts lovers. The library's collection development policy for books will be a useful starting point for planning the video collection as well.

TECHNICAL ASPECTS

In moving to the consideration of the technical aspects of film, we reach the heart of the difference in evaluating print and motion pictures. The skillful combination of visuals and sound is the true art and craft of filmmaking. In a film production, the director is usually the "author" of the work, but rarely performs all of the tasks alone. The ability to combine all of the elements skillfully is an essential part of the art of film.

There is often confusion about the tasks of filmmaking. The producer is the person responsible for the overall project. The producer raises the money, runs the business aspects of the production, and hires the director. While the producer supervises the overall production, the director is responsible for the actual production itself, supervising all aspects of preparation, writing, filming, and editing. Thus, the director is usually considered the "author." Often, especially in documentary filmmaking, there is a producer/director. In large budget features and network television there is usually a confusing array of credits for "executive producers," "line producers," "second unit director," etc. But, as a rule of thumb, the producer is the businessperson, while the director is the artistic guide; the person who brings together the elements of writing, visuals, sound, and editing into a (hopefully) cohesive whole.

VISUALS

From the very first motion pictures shot with one stationary camera, full of flickers and blurs, to the latest high-tech movies with upside down, sideways, continually moving multiple cameras (often full of purposeful flickers and blurs) cinematography has been key to the art of filmmaking. In many ways we have become inured to good cinematography. By watching mainstream feature films and network television we take for granted something that is more difficult than most of us realize. We have come to expect superb photography. It is usually only when we see something truly amazing that we even notice it. Or, if we have the experience of shooting home videos ourselves, we come to appreciate how difficult it really is.

The importance of the cinematography in evaluating a video for purchase will vary according to its importance to the production. A straightforward informational piece does not call for imaginative movement or "arty" shots. They may, in fact, be distracting. But one really should expect footage to be in focus, visuals neither under- nor over-exposed, figures in the frame without the tops of the heads missing, etc.

Of course, some of these basics have to be considered in context. Some of the most exciting social documentaries are shot with handheld cameras under less than ideal conditions. The immediacy of the events being depicted should be taken into consideration, as should the filmmaker's "style." For example, it is ironic that black-and-white photography is back in style. Long considered "old-fashioned" because of the brilliant color film that is available, many of us who love the movies also appreciate the art of good cinematography in black-and-white. Far from making a film look "cheap," black-and-white photography now often costs more to produce. ("Everything old is new again.")

Some of the most creative filmmaking breaks supposed "rules" by stretching the boundaries. Film and video artists use the medium as a canvas. All of these considerations should go into the evaluation of materials. In other words, the cinematography in each work should be considered in the context of its purpose.

SOUND

While visuals are, of course, the most noticeable aspect of a work on film, sound is just as important in creating a quality work. The first thing to remember is that a good soundtrack is an integration of elements, and their skillful blending, and often unobtrusiveness, is the key.

In many films, especially feature films, there are at least three soundtracks running simultaneously and in sync. First is the dialogue track, the one carrying the characters' conversations, and/or the narration. Then there is the sound effects' track—the sounds a viewer would expect to hear in the background of the scene being depicted. Sound effects editing is an art of its own. For example, a nineteenth century street scene might include a horse and buggy traveling down a street behind two actors in conversation. A good sound effects editor will consider how the street is paved (a cobbled street will sound different than a dirt street), what shoes the horse would be wearing and how they would sound, and the weight and type of the buggy. Is there a snap of a whip? A command to the horse from the driver?

Then, of course, there is the music track, which can either add immeasurably to a film's emotional and aesthetic impact, or be irritatingly distracting. As with sound effects, often the sign of the best work is its invisibility. A musical track is judged on appropriateness to the purpose of the work, as well as clarity. A more subjective consideration is the amount of music used. I, personally, can be driven to distraction by wall-to-wall music in informational videos, for example. Music tracks are like conversation—noise to fill silence to no purpose is annoying. And often that type of generic music seems to be only a gathering of notes without a theme.

The art of sound consists in the mixing of these various tracks into a cohesive whole. Almost always in feature films the sound effects and dialogue are mixed separately. It is simply too difficult to make dialogue understandable over natural street sounds in an outside scene, for example.

In documentary filmmaking, the natural sounds are very often key to the piece. As with cinematography, the context of the work should be considered equally to the fidelity of the sound. Yet comprehensibility is important to every video work. It loses impact if the message comes across as garbled or unintelligible.

EDITING

Another essential craft of filmmaking is editing. Most of the art of film, in fact, is created in the editing room after shooting is completed. It is in the editing process that all of the elements of the film are brought together and mixed into the final work. This is usually done by a professional film editor, in conjunction with the director.

At the end of shooting a film, whether fiction feature, documentary, or educational, there is always a great deal of raw footage. Organizing it, selecting what to keep and what to abandon ("the face on the cutting room floor" of legend), mixing it with the soundtracks—this is what makes a film.

Good editing is usually invisible. We are often aware of squirming when a scene goes on and on, or when an interview in a documentary is inane or repetitive. These are signs of bad editing. Yet we are less aware of the quick cutting back and forth between the shark, the unsuspecting swimmer, the boat, and the calm scene on the beach that got our hearts pounding in *Jaws*, for example. Add the appropriately unsettling music and sounds of lapping water, and you have an example of truly skillful editing. The same can be said of a documentary that skillfully mixes interesting and insightful interviews with appropriate footage, well-selected music and skillfully read, articulate narration. Such an example familiar to most would be Ken Burns' "Civil War" series. Making a compelling, seamless, and dramatic presentation from still photographs and interviews shows amazing skill.

Before leaving the section on technical aspects, it is important to say something about acting, as well. All of us have enough experience with watching films and television to be able to distinguish between good and bad acting. This is truly a collaborative effort between performer and director. Additionally, it is my opinion that narration is an often overlooked element that can make or break a non-fiction work. Voice quality and timbre are important, as is expressiveness and casting the appropriate voice for the script being read.

USAGE

Unlike the Kaels and Eberts of the world, the librarian evaluating motion pictures for libraries has an additional consideration beyond those already discussed: how the program can be used.

For a public librarian this again depends on the mission of the library. A collection of popular features, arts, and how-tos may be just the thing for a popular library. If the library has any type of research or academic support responsibility, then a wider consideration of usage is called for.

For schools, colleges, and those public libraries with research responsibilities, there are some simple guidelines for evaluating the usefulness of a program for the library's collection. First, does the program achieve its stated purpose? In most cases, videos produced for the educational market specifically will offer this information in its materials accompanying the video. This includes age level and areas of study. With commercial tapes this is not always as easy, as marketers often claim that a program is for "everyone," if they indicate an intended audience at all. In evaluating for usage, establishing the age level is accomplished by such indicators as the vocabulary used in the program, as well as the level of complexity of concepts in the program. A helpful tool for those selecting material for the K-12 age group in schools is the textbook correlation which some educational distributors provide with their classroom instructional videos. These charts match concepts in the program with the lessons on these same concepts in the major textbook series.

In selecting for classroom use, the rules on objectivity are also somewhat different than in selecting for a general audience, as was discussed above. While point-of-view is still a plus for making a good program, and for generating thinking and discussion, if a program is going to be used in a classroom, any bias should be recognized and acknowledged.

In evaluating a program for its usefulness, particularly in a school setting, it is even more important than with a general audience evaluation to consider whether or not the program will maintain interest in the intended audience. A long program, no matter how skillfully crafted, is usually not appropriate for primary grade students, for example. And, it cannot be emphasized too often, consider if this is a good use of the medium. Does the combining of visuals and sound with content make sense to teach the material being presented? Will this work with other materials, such as print and audio, to teach the subject at hand? How will it fit in the overall library collection?

CONCLUSION

There is one last consideration before moving away from the evaluation process. In the discussion above I deliberately have not mentioned book adaptations. One of the worst possible standards for evaluating a video is whether or not it is based on a book, and, if so, whether or not it is "true" to the original. Videos should stand on their own as works of art or information. It is an insult to the medium to suggest that a video work only has legitimacy if it "leads to reading."

Some of the best children's videos, for example, are book-based. The delightful work from Weston Woods (Children's Circle on the consumer market) is a fine example of how picture books can be enhanced by meticulous animation mixed with skillful sound and narration. The fact that they are book-based is a plus, but not their reason for being. They are, first, good films.

This should always be the criterion. Is any version of *War and Peace* as good as the book? No. Yet, especially with today's popular fiction, a thriller or romance is so often obviously a "pre-screenplay" (John Grisham comes to mind) that the filmed version is often better. Maybe these works aren't "great film," but they are "good movies." Not everything (and this is particularly true for children) has to be educational. Having fun is okay, too.

When all is said and done, the evaluation of video is subjective. Remember the "hair-on-the-arms-standing-on-end" syndrome. Nothing replaces lots of concentrated viewing in developing skill in video selection. It is an emotional art form, and when it is done well it evokes strong emotion—laughter, tears, anger, or lingering thought. See the appendix for two useful tools for video evaluation in libraries. One is the excellent criteria for evaluation used by reviewers for *Booklist*. The other is a sample video evaluation form for librarians.

3 VIDEO SELECTION AND ACQUISITIONS

Using the hints discussed in the last chapter, anyone evaluating video for library purchase should be able to make informed choices based on viewing. While in the best of all possible worlds, every book would be read before purchase, and every video viewed, in the real world most purchases must be made based on reviews, catalogs, and the reputation of the author/publisher/producer/filmmaker. Additionally, the library user, whether a member of the public or a teacher or professor, needs information to make informed choices about titles in the collection.

REVIEWS AND REFERENCE

In this chapter we will consider the tools available to the librarian for acquisition and to the library user for selection. This will include *professional library reviews*, *consumer reviews*, and *video reference works*. The chapter will include only the most essential and broad-based works available. The bibliography at the end of the chapter will also include more specialized works.

PROFESSIONAL LIBRARY REVIEWS

A number of journals in the library field include some reviews of video material. The ones listed here are the best in terms of the breadth of coverage and the direct relevance to library video collections in all types of libraries.

Booklist. 50 E. Huron St., Chicago, IL 60611; semi-monthly.

This long-time leader in the field of library reviewing is published by the American Library Association. The Audiovisual Media section reviews a good number of nonfiction video titles in each issue. *Booklist* has the distinct strength of offering reviews by full-time staff members supported by some outside reviewers. All are professional librarians, and reviews are written with a keen eye on how each title will fit in a library's collection, and addresses appropriateness for age level and type of library. Reviews are printed only for titles recommended for purchase. There are also periodic helpful subject lists, such as AIDS education. A helpful feature is cataloging and classification information for each title reviewed.

Children's Video Report. P.O. Box 3228, Princeton, NJ 08543-3228; 8x yr.

While not a library publication *per se*, this excellent publication's approach to video is very compatible with library standards for purchase. Reviews, while limited in number, are comprehensive and dependable. The editor has a good feel for the needs of libraries, and publishes helpful articles and special videographies.

Library Journal. 245 W. 17th St., New York, NY 10011; semimonthly.

As with their book review section, the *LJ* video reviews are written by field reviewers. A substantial number of titles are covered, with library collections clearly in mind. Field reviewers are both a strength and a weakness. While the general level remains high through editorial diligence, it is difficult to assess an individual reviewer's expertise and/or bias. All the titles reviewed are at the adult level.

School Library Journal. 245 W. 17th St., New York, NY 10011; monthly.

As with its sister publication, *Library Journal*, this tried-and-true publication relies on field reviewers. A good source for school library reviews, as well as children's video in general.

Science Books and Films. American Association for the Advancement of Science, P.O. Box 3000, Department SBF, Denville, NJ 07834; 9x yr.

This excellent review journal is particularly helpful for school libraries purchasing for curriculum collections. While the title suggests pure science, the reviews also cover technology and the social sciences. A good choice, too, for public libraries for selecting nonfiction titles in the sciences.

Video Librarian. P.O. Box 2725, Bremerton, WA 98310; monthly.

Editor/publisher Randy Pitman has accomplished the nearly impossible—creating a review journal that is hard to put down. Aimed specifically at public libraries (though school and academic librarians will find guidance, too), all age groups and subject areas are covered. The reviews (largely written by Pitman himself) are authoritative, helpful, and often funny. His background as a video librarian in a public library make this a highly professional, as well as highly entertaining, journal.

A few years ago a national survey of libraries with video collections contained the surprising and disturbing fact that the most common source cited by librarians in selecting videos for purchase was distributor catalogs rather than professional review sources. While one's professional sensibilities shrink from such a concept, it is also important to discuss some helpful selection sources from distributors. Keeping in mind that the underlying purpose of such publications is to get you to purchase what's included, used in conjunction with professional reviews these publications can be of real assistance.

Baker & Taylor Video Alert. 2709 Water Ridge Parkway, Charlotte, NC 28217. This publication is a good source of information about which videos are being released on the home market. It includes both feature films and nonfiction popular documentaries, children's videos, and how-tos. Written for the library market, there is also helpful editorial content, such as subject lists and recommended featured titles for special events and holidays.

Facets Video Catalogue. 1517 W. Fullerton Ave., Chicago, IL 60614. This Chicago-based exhibitor and distributor is an excellent source for alternative fiction and nonfiction videos. Particularly strong in the area of foreign productions, this is an essential source for libraries, and a helpful guide both for purchase and as a reference tool on the independent and foreign film market.

Ingram Video Update. One Ingram Blvd., La Vergne, TN 37086-1986. This catalog from a major book and video jobber is designed for the library market, and alerts customers to new releases particularly appropriate for library collections.

PBS Video News. 1320 Braddock Place, Alexandria, VA 22314-1698. A newsletter for library customers, this periodic publication is useful for news about upcoming public television programming and videocassette availability. This is an example of a type of newsletter that appears from time to time from various library video distributors.

CONSUMER REVIEWS

Trying to keep up with current publications in the consumer video field can be very frustrating. It would be impossible to count the number of publications with the word "Video" in the title that have gone in and out of business in the last decade. Those listed below are the ones most often mentioned as useful by working video librarians. Subscription prices are listed because some of the best are also out of reach for many smaller libraries. Additionally, every newspaper of any size offers some type of reviewing of home video releases.

Billboard, 1515 Broadway, New York, NY 10036. ($225 yr.) This weekly is a Bible for the "biz" in "show biz." It is very useful for charting trends in consumer tastes.

Premiere, K-III Magazine Corporation, 2 Park Ave., New York, NY 10016. ($18 yr.) Particularly good for tracking what mainstream movies are in the pipeline and being released; it also reviews home video releases.

Variety, 475 Park Ave. South, New York, NY 10019. ($149 yr.) The best source for entertainment news, it also does a reasonable job of reviewing new consumer video releases.

Video Business, 825 Seventh Ave., New York, NY 10019. ($70 yr.) This and the title that follows are excellent choices because they not only offer home video reviews, but also helpful statistics and collection management tips from the perspective of the video store.

Video Store, 1700 E. Dyer Rd., Suite 250, Santa Ana, CA 92705. ($48 yr.) See above.

VIDEO REFERENCE

There are a few reference works that are valuable for title identification, as well as distributor and price information. Again, only the most key are listed here. Additionally, many of these works are becoming available online.

Bowker's Complete Video Directory. New York, R. R. Bowker. This multi-volume work is getting better as their database expands, but is still most useful for feature films. It, like other consumer publications, falls short in the area of subject access to titles.

Educational Film and Video Locator of the Consortium of College and University Media Centers. New York, R. R. Bowker. A good source for locating educational video titles.

Film and Video Finder. Albuquerque, NM, Access Information. Formerly *NICEM Index*, this work attempts to be comprehensive in its listing of educational videos. Available in CD-ROM, and also as *A-V Online*.

The Video Source Book. Detroit, Gale Research. 1995. A comprehensive listing of videos currently on the market. Like *Bowker* above, it suffers from lack of subject access.

A Quick Guide to Movie Guides

Movie guides serve at least two useful functions in a library. First, guides can be used for quick reference to answer user inquiries about films, directors, actors, etc. Secondly, and probably most important, for a public library feature film collection, consumer guides located near the video collections can be used by borrowers to get ideas about what to check out, and to check ratings and reviews for "appropriateness" for their viewing. This can be invaluable in helping library staff to stay out of the role of censor or interpreter of MPAA ratings. The following quick reference examines some major consumer guides with these criteria in mind.

Ebert, Roger. *Roger Ebert's Video Companion*. Kansas City, Andrews and McMeel, annual.
At 1300 entries, this is a very selective guide, which includes intelligent reviews and features essays on film topics and profiles of important actors, directors, etc. Rates on a one–four basis, has a good representation of foreign films and some documentaries, and includes MPAA ratings.

Elley, Derek, ed. *Variety Movie Guide*. London, Hamly, annual.
This single volume is selected and edited from the twenty-two-volume *Variety Film Reviews*, which includes movies released since 1907. At 7500 entries there is good representation of films from both the U.S. and U.K. Foreign films are not well represented, and because of its British origin, MPAA ratings are not included. Well written reviews, Academy Award listings, and laserdisc availability are its strengths.

Maltin, Leonard. *Leonard Maltin's Movie and Video Guide*. Plume/Penguin, annual.
At 19,000 short entries, this may be the most useful guide for borrowers for quick reference. An excellent representation of foreign, documentary, as well as mainstream popular films. A one–four star rating system and MPAA ratings included. Also available on computer disc.

Martin, Mick and Marsha Porter. *Video Movie Guide*. Ballantine, annual.
Another extremely useful quick reference guide for borrowers. Short paragraph descriptions of 15,000 films include not only MPAA ratings, but the reason (violence, sexual content) for the rating. A one–four star rating system is supplemented by a turkey symbol for real stinkers. Arranged by genre, there are sections on foreign films, documentaries, as well as an alphabetical index.

Pallot, James, et. al. *The Movie Guide*, 2nd ed. Perigee, 1995.
Selected and condensed from the monumental multi-volume *Motion Picture Guide*, this one-volume paperback is a good selective source. Includes a one–four star rating system, good alternative title information and some foreign films. Also includes MPAA ratings.

Video Hound's Golden Video Retriever. Detroit, Visible Ink Press, annual
Without doubt, this guide is the most fun. But it also includes a great deal of very valuable information. 22,000 entries include a one–four "bone" rating system, 4700 foreign film listings, awards listings, and MPAA ratings. It features some very useful indexes, such as directors, variant titles, and song titles, as well as "kibbles," fun lists such as "MGM musicals," "chases," and "cave people."

Walker, John ed. *Halliwell's Film Guide*. Harper Perennial.

This annual British publication is well-regarded in the film community. Very brief plot descriptions are supplemented with extensive cast and crew credits and awards. Includes a good listing of foreign films. Provides a one–four star rating system. Because it is British, MPAA ratings are not included.

Note: Many guides are now available in CD-ROM versions.

ACQUIRING VIDEOS

There is no question that the video business is confusing and frustrating for librarians. It seems it should work very much like the book business, and on the surface this is true. But there are many exceptions, including whole marketing initiatives that operate unlike any segment of the print business. One reason for the confusion is that the videocassette "sell-through" (an industry tag) business is really two converging businesses coming from two very different directions—the consumer video business, which is very like the book business, and often conducted by the same people; and the independent and alternative video business, which is an outgrowth of the 16mm educational film business.

The video business itself is divided into two distinct segments—video rental and video sell-through. The video rental business is one of the most incredible business stories of all time. In 1980 a video rental store was unknown; by 1985 there was a "Mom and Pop" store on every corner. By 1990 giant video chains were dominating a multi-billion dollar industry.

But it is the sell-through market that directly effects libraries. This, too, is broken down into three segments: *wholesalers*, *retailers*, and *single source distributors*. We will discuss each of these in turn, as well as talk about *duplication licensing*.

How does a video get into distribution? For the most part, it depends on its intended audience and its potential market. Usually, the producer of the work controls its copyright and arranges the assignment of rights. In this way, the video business is different than the book business. For example, a mainstream feature film will be distributed to theaters in the U.S. There will often be a separate distribution deal for foreign theatrical showings. Then there will be home video rights, television rights, foreign television rights, and nontheatrical rights (college campus screenings, etc.). In some cases, there will also be educational rights. In other words, one movie can have multiple contracts assigned for various types of distribution. A library can encounter problems with this when, for example, a collection is being used for home circulation, library programs, community programs, and educational use. We will explore this minefield in more detail when we discuss copyright law.

Independent and alternative materials tend to be handled by fewer contractors, because the audience is seen to be more limited, and the emphasis is on the educational and library market. These works, however, do often have separate television distribution, and may even have both educational and home video distributors. Yes, it is confusing!

WHOLESALERS

These vendors, also called "jobbers" in the trade, offer one-stop shopping for theatrical movies and mainstream home video programs. The two best known of these are Baker & Taylor and Ingram. Both are well-known as major suppliers of books to libraries. When video became an important part of library collections, these suppliers moved in to fill the need. The majority of their video sales isn't to libraries, however, but to video stores. The resulting large volume of business these suppliers do, however, is of great advantage to libraries because of the low prices they can offer.

Like books, videos are sold at wholesale prices. Libraries have the added advantage, in many cases, of being able to add video titles to the library's book order to increase their discounts even further. Additionally, all of the major library wholesalers offer convenient electronic ordering.

While Baker & Taylor and Ingram are certainly the best-known and most frequently used, they are not the only players in the video wholesaling business. These wholesalers, along with Bro-Dart and others, offer full service to libraries, including in many cases, cataloging and packaging services. Another company, Professional Media Services, is exclusively a library audiovisual wholesaler, and specializes in the location of titles and cataloging services.

Another type of wholesaler is known as a "rack jobber." This business specializes in stocking the shelves of large chain stores, such as K-Mart and Target. The videos are selected by type, rather than by individual title, and often include "sale" items, such as remainders and cheap copies of public domain movies. The quality of these tapes varies significantly, both in content and technical considerations. For example, a movie in public domain can be made even cheaper by using extended play tapes, which while making manufacturing cheaper, also makes picture quality problematic.

RETAILERS

Retailers, like wholesalers, offer a wide range of videotapes for sale to libraries. While deep discounts are not included, these companies offer customer service tailored to libraries and schools, and catalogs of tapes gathered from many sources that are especially appropriate for the library and school market. This can be a great boon to a busy library staff without someone with time to carefully select from the wide range of materials available. A good example is the Library Video Company, which has created a good subject-based video catalog for libraries, drawing from many quality sources. They have also recently begun producing excellent classroom instructional videos.

Additionally, for a library feature film collection, used video services can be a boon. While one must be careful to check the tapes, a good way to fill in the collection of popular features is to purchase used tapes, which come mostly from video stores. The shelf life of a hot new title is usually not more than six weeks in the video business. The way video stores work is exactly the opposite of the way libraries work. They buy the newest titles in great quantity, and then in a few weeks are through with them. A library looking for a broad-based collection can pick up many titles this way at a great savings.

Another method for acquiring used titles is to develop a good relationship with a local video store owner and buy used tapes directly from the store when the demand has lessened. This is excellent public relations in a field where library-commercial relationships have not always been cordial.

SINGLE SOURCE DISTRIBUTION

The purchase sources for video we have been discussing up to this point are all non-exclusive distributors. This means they carry videos from many different producers, and the same titles will be found in many catalogs. In other words, you will find a Children's Circle title like "Really Rosie" in many different catalogs.

Single source distribution of video, an outgrowth of the educational film business, works very differently. In its purest form, a producer will sign an exclusive contract for school and library distribution with a distributor specializing in this field. No other source will offer this particular title to schools and libraries. These videos are often the alternative and special, with a small potential for home video purchase. Often their only outlet, except for public and cable television, will be libraries and schools. Because of their uniqueness and small market potential, these titles, while often the most interesting and original, are also expensive. This means that the deep discounting that is necessary for them to be included in the large wholesaler catalogs is simply not feasible for either party.

As we have seen, there are some real advantages to purchasing from these distributors.

- Some of the most interesting and original work is available only from these sources.
- Voices and viewpoints not heard in the mainstream media are included in these collections.
- They almost always come with public performance rights included, which means they can be used for library and community programming; and;
- they often come with study materials which make them valuable for classroom use.

A list of some single source distributors you might want to consider for acquisition of videocassettes is at the end of this chapter.

Additionally, since the mid-1980s, there have been several opportunities for public libraries to purchase independent programming at reduced prices through projects sponsored by private foundations. In the late 1980s these included the MacArthur Video Classics project and the ALA-Carnegie Quality Video for Youth project. Currently, National Video Resources, an initiative of the Rockefeller Foundation, is sponsoring *VideoForum*, an excellent occasional publication. Centering around a theme (Native Americans, Latino culture, health issues), essays are supported by a skillfully curated collection of videos that are then made available at greatly reduced prices for an extended period after the publication. Public libraries receive *VideoForum* free of charge. (Write to National Video Resources, 73 Spring Street, New York, NY 10012). While independent productions still tend to cost more than home video, the prices are steadily declining, and their benefit to the potential audience often outweighs the extra cost.

OFF-AIR TAPING AND DUPLICATION LICENSING

Another source for acquiring video, especially for schools, is by off-air taping of television programming, and/or purchasing licenses to duplicate single copies. While at first glance this would seem a simple and inexpensive way to build a video collection, it is a practice that requires both attention to detail and a good working knowledge of the copyright law.

At the simplest level is the purchase of duplication licenses. This means that if a library needs several copies of the same program, it is often possible to negotiate with an educational distributor to purchase one copy and then pay a reduced rate for additional copies the library manufactures itself. The practice is widespread in school media centers, and is very convenient when many teachers are asking for the same program at the same time. I do not recommend this practice for most public libraries. For one thing, sophisticated equipment and knowledgeable staff are essential in order to make satisfactory copies. Additionally, in a public library browsing collection, those plain black boxes and typed labels are deadly. Since video prices are steadily dropping, it is usually better just to purchase two or more original copies from the distributor.

As for off-air taping, again school and academic libraries will find this practice more useful than public libraries. Be sure to review the section on the copyright law (pages 59–66) for details, but in a nutshell, there are only certain exceptions under which programming may be taped off the air and then used for anything but sitting privately in your own living room and viewing it. And these exceptions are usually more applicable to the classroom. A *teacher* may tape a program off the air, but

- must register the intent to do so;
- may only show the program *twice* during the first ten days;
- may then keep the tape for another thirty-five days for purchase consideration, and then;
- *must erase it.*

Most school districts and college campuses have developed policies and forms for complying with these requirements. For the most part, the complicated compliance requirements are not worth it for public libraries, except in very special circumstances. If one cares about the quality of the image and sound, second generation tapes are not only illegal, they are inferior.

Selection Shortcuts

In many libraries video selection must be done by staff with many other duties to perform. Below are some suggested strategies for making the best use of "the experts" in choosing quality programming.

1. Watch the newspapers for lists of major awards:
   - Academy Awards
   - Emmys
   - Independent Spirit Awards (independent features)
   - Sundance Film Festival (independent features)
   - ACE Awards (cable television)

2. Read and follow the advice of:
   Booklist (50 E. Huron, Chicago, IL 60611)
   Video Librarian (P.O. Box 2725, Bremerton, WA 98310)

3. Obtain these American Library Association lists each year by calling 1-800-545-2433:
   Notable Films and Videos for Children and the Andrew Carnegie Medal for Excellence in Children's Video (Association for Library Service to Children)
   Selected Films and Videos for Young Adults (Young Adult Library Service Association)

4. Subscribe to *Parent's Choice*. (Parent's Choice Awards), (Box 185, Waban, MA 02168)

5. Join the Coalition for Quality Children's Video to receive their directory. (545 Cordova Rd., Suite 456, Santa Fe, NM 87501)

STAFF PURCHASE RESPONSIBILITY

Perhaps one of the most difficult questions to answer in an era of changing technologies and library and media center organization, is who should have the final authority in the acquisition of video. In the days of film libraries it was almost always the audiovisual specialist, often with the input from a committee of subject and age-group specialists. Whether for better or worse, the era of the preview committee taking time to fully screen every possible title for inclusion in the library is long gone. Video selection is now much more like book selection, with specialists choosing materials through reviews, advertising and respected producers. But the question still remains, who will have the authority to make purchase decisions?

In many libraries today, the person in charge of overall collection development will carry the responsibility for selecting materials regardless of format. In larger libraries, collection development subject specialists will have this responsibility. In libraries where there is a separate video department, the question arises whether the video librarian (or media specialist in a school) or specialist (youth services, business, arts) should have this responsibility.

There is no question that in public libraries, at least, the trend is towards subject collection development specialists who select for all formats. The concern expressed by many in the video field regarding this practice has to do with whether those assigned the responsibility have the same background and experience with the visual formats as they do with print. Building a quality video collection (whether it is a separate department or integrated with print) is much more than simply picking out familiar-sounding titles from distributor catalogs. A good knowledge of film technique, genres, film history, and filmmakers is also highly desirable. Perhaps the best system is one in which subject specialists make recommendations based on subject matter, accuracy, and appropriateness, while a video specialist keeps a keen eye on technical quality and filling gaps that are important from the standpoint of filmmaking.

COOPERATIVE PURCHASING

While new formats and new technologies have brought new excitement to the library field, there is also no question that there are enormous challenges attached—not the least of which is how to make static or declining library budgets cover current demands and at the same time add new formats and services.

One solution being adopted by many libraries of all types is cooperative purchasing. Purchasing cooperatives, consortia, and circuits have long been a mainstay of library audiovisual service. Because of the relative high cost of 16mm films, many libraries participated in some type of cooperative service in the 1960s and 1970s. While many of these disappeared or reduced their services with the advent of home video, in recent years cooperative video purchasing has made a comeback.

There are two main models for shared resources, the *cooperative or consortium* and the *circuit*. The cooperative or consortium model libraries join together to purchase materials and save through an economy of scale. Usually, libraries then keep the videos they have purchased in this manner. In the circuit model, a central administrative unit (often a system headquarters) acts as administrator. Member libraries pay a set amount into a central pool. After purchases are made, videos are divided into packets that are rotated to member libraries, often for one-to-two month periods. This method works particularly well for smaller libraries with limited resources.

Cooperative purchasing can have three main advantages for libraries: *favorable pricing for participating libraries*, *sharing of administrative and operational tasks*, and *opportunity to enhance collection diversity*.

FAVORABLE PRICING

The primary goal of cooperative purchasing is to offer more videocassettes to library users for less money, especially in the area of independent and alternative filmmaking. Cooperative purchasing makes possible discount negotiation usually even with the smallest single-source distributors. Of course, it is important that the "cooperation" extend to the distributors as well. While libraries will be looking for the maximum discount, distributors must also be allowed to make some profit so that more programs will be forthcoming.

There is no rule about what type of discount can be expected, but such considerations as all ordered copies on one invoice, shipping to a single address, etc., can achieve the deepest discounts. Discounts tend to be lower for programs that are already low-priced (under $50).

SHARING OF ADMINISTRATIVE AND OPERATIONAL TASKS

Video ordering can be a time-consuming task, especially when dealing with the single-source distributors. By pooling their resources, libraries can streamline the process through centralization of the operation. This works best, of course, where library systems already have shared services in place, though this is not essential.

Cooperatives work in different ways to accomplish economical operations. In some cases, orders are gathered and then sent in a single batch to a distributor. In other cases, orders may go separately to the distributor, but are all shipped to one location. Technical processing may or may not be included. In the case of circuits, rotation of the collection needs to be worked out and implemented.

ENHANCING COLLECTION DIVERSITY

Of equal importance to the financial considerations of cooperative buying is the opportunity for libraries to build diverse and specialized collections. With the increased buying power offered by cooperation, libraries are able to build better collections. This may take the form of special collections, where an individual library, through local interest or need, purchases heavily in a specialization, e.g., opera, AIDS education, or topics of local import. Ideally a library will share its collection with others via interlibrary loan. However, if this is not possible, the library still gains from belonging to a cooperative by being able to purchase nonspecialized materials less expensively, thus leaving more funds for its special collections.

By the same token, other members of a cooperative will gain by being able to access specialized materials for their users. Each member, of course, must make a contribution, either through funding or offering of special materials to all.

CONCLUSION

Obviously, buying through consortia is an excellent acquisition strategy. So, why isn't everybody doing it? Experience has shown that in addition to great advantages there are real barriers to overcome. They are obviously not insurmountable, since some very successful consortia are thriving, but it is very important to consider them before attempting to launch a buying group.

Probably the greatest barrier for every buying cooperative is in satisfying all of the various policy and operational procedures of individual members. No consortium can succeed without a thoroughgoing initial process for working out details. Equally important is establishing in advance who will do the actual work. It is true that "time is money," and there must be an honest examination of whether there is an institution or individual who can realistically accomplish the time-consuming tasks demanded.

For a more detailed description of consortium models, see the appendix.

SELECTED SOURCES FOR VIDEO PURCHASE

Wholesalers and Retailers

Baker & Taylor, 501 S. Gladiolus, Momence, IL 60954. (800) 435-5111

Bro-Dart, 500 Arch St., Williamsport, PA 17705. (800) 233-8467

Ingram Library Services, P.O. Box 3006, La Vergne, TN 37086-1986. (615) 793-5000

Library Video Company, P.O. Box 110, Bala Cynwyd, PA 19004. (800) 843-3620

Professional Media Services Corporation, 19122 S. Vermont Ave., Gardena, CA 90248. (800) 223-7672

SINGLE SOURCE DISTRIBUTORS:

Educational/Instructional

AIMS Media, 9710 DeSoto Ave., Chatsworth, CA 91311-4409. (800) 773-4300; (818) 773-4300

Altschul Group, 1560 Sherman Ave., Evanston, IL 60201. (800) 323-9084; (708) 328-6700

Ambrose Video Publishing, 381 Park Avenue South, New York, NY 10016. (212) 696-4545

Annenberg/CPB Collection, P.O. Box 2345, South Barrington, VT 05407-2345. (800) LEARNER

Barr Films, 12801 Schabarum Ave., Irwindale, CA 91706-7878. (800) 234-7878; (818) 338-7878

Bullfrog Films, P.O. Box 149, Oley, PA 19547. (800) 543-FROG

Carousel Film & Video, 260 5th Avenue, New York, NY 10001. (212) 683-1660

Chip Taylor Communications, 15 Spollet Drive, Derry, NH 03038. (800) 876-CHIP; (603) 434-9262

Churchill Media, 6901 Woodley Dr., Van Nuys, CA 91406; (800) 334-7830

Coronet/MTI, 108 Wilmot Rd., Deerfield, IL 60015; (800) 777-8100

Films for the Humanities and Sciences, P.O. Box 2053, Princeton, NJ 08543. (800) 257-5126

Films, Inc., 5547 N. Ravenswood, Chicago, IL 60640-1199. (312) 878-2600

Landmark Films, 3450 Slade Run Dr., Falls Church, VA 22042. (800) 342-4336; (703) 241-2030

Lucerne Media, 37 Ground Pine Rd., Morris Plains, NJ 07950. (800) 341-2293; (201) 538-1401

PBS Video, 1320 Braddock Pl., Alexandria, VA 22314-1698. (703) 739-5380

Phoenix/BFA Films, 2349 Chaffee Dr., St. Louis, MO 63146. (800) 221-1274

Pyramid Film & Video, P.O. Box 1048, Santa Monica, CA 90406. (800) 421-2304; (310) 828-7577

Weston Woods Studios, 389 Newtown Turnpike, Weston, CT 06883. (203) 226-3355

Independent/Alternative

Appalshop Film & Video, 306 Madison St., Whitesburg, KY 41858. (800) 545-7467; (606) 633-0108

California Newsreel, 149 9th St., San Francisco, CA 94103. (415) 621-6196

Cinema Guild, 1697 Broadway, New York, NY 10019. (212) 246-5522

Cross Current Media, 346 9th St., San Francisco, CA 94103. (415) 552-9550

Direct Cinema, P.O. Box 10003, Santa Monica, CA 90410-9003. (800) 345-6748

Electronic Arts Intermix, 536 Broadway, 9th Floor, New York, NY 10019. (212) 966-4605

Fanlight Productions, 47 Halifax St., Boston, MA 02130. (617) 524-0980

Filmakers Library, 124 E. 40th St., New York, NY 10016. (212) 808-4980

First Run/Icarus Films, 200 Park Ave. South, Suite 1319, New York, NY 10003. (800) 876-1710

Flower Films and Video, 10341 San Pablo Ave., El Cerrito, CA 94530. (510) 525-0942

William Greaves Productions, 230 W. 55th St., New York, NY 10019. (800) 874-8314

Museum of Modern Art Circulating Film and Video Library, 11 W. 53rd St., New York, NY 10019. (212) 708-9530

National Film Board of Canada, 1251 Avenue of the Americas, 16th Floor, New York, NY 10020-1173. (212) 586-5131

NAPBC (Native American Public Broadcasting Consortium), P.O. Box 83111, Lincoln, NE 68501. (402) 472-3522

New Day Films, 121 W. 27 St., Suite 902, New York, NY 10001. (212) 645-8210

New Yorker Video, 16 W. 61st St., New York, NY 10023. (212) 247-6110

Third World Newsreel, 335 W. 38th St., New York, NY 10018. (212) 947-9277

Women Make Movies, 225 Lafayette St., Suite 212, New York, NY 10012. (212) 925-0606

BIBLIOGRAPHY

Kemp, Betty. *School Library and Media Center Acquisitions Policies and Procedures*. Phoenix, AZ, Oryx Press, 1987.

Scholtz, James. *Video Acquisitions and Cataloging: A Handbook*. Westport, CT, Greenwood Press, 1995.

4 VIDEO COLLECTION DEVELOPMENT POLICIES

In this section we will deal with video in the context of the entire library collection. This means, above all, having clear written policies about how video fits in the collection as well as how it will be selected, acquired, processed, managed, and circulated. One sure way to ensure that a quality collection is built is to develop and carry out sound policies.

Many librarians have been tempted to just add the word "video" to their library's overall collection development policy. While this takes care of certain aspects, there are others that need to be considered and developed with video specifically in mind. This does not mean that the library necessarily needs to have a completely separate document for video. In fact, incorporating video into the overall collection development policy statement strengthens the entire collection. There are, however, some unique considerations for video, and we will treat these in detail in this chapter.

SURVEYING THE COMMUNITY

While this book is not a blueprint for writing an overall library collection development policy, it is important to note that the policy needs to begin with a mission statement reflecting the demographics of the community or institution being served.

If the population served is in a school or academic setting, the mission will most likely be to support the curriculum of the institution. Considerations will be the balance between core curriculum needs and supplemental and recreational materials that might be included. The public library has a slightly more complex decision about its mission statement, and will probably use the Public Library Association's guidelines for developing its mission statement.

So how does video fit into this framework? The demographics of a community or user base is an important consideration about what size the video collection should be in proportion to the entire library collection, as well as what materials should be chosen, what age levels served, etc.

In considering demographics when developing a video collection, these are some pieces of information that will be the most useful:

— size of the population (or student body);

— age groups served;

— ethnic and racial makeup and percentages of the total population;

— languages spoken; and

— community economic base (schools' libraries should also consider the curriculum offered).

For example, video may be a truly basic library resource in a community with a large number of members with low reading skills. As I have stated before, in this situation videocassettes may be an essential tool for basic information. In other communities, performances of plays, ballets, and operas may appeal to a large segment of a population with a strong interest in the arts. Parenting, health issues, and an emphasis on quality children's materials may be the focus for a population with a large number of young families. In other words, deciding what type of videos are purchased, and what percentage of the overall materials they should constitute, is a decision directly affected by the population demographics and stated mission of the library.

WORKING WITH YOUR GOVERNING BODY

Whether the library's governing body is a school board or a library board, the key to building a quality collection is in support from that body, both in the form of budget allocations and in support for the collection and the role it will serve in the library's collection. This is particularly important when building a video collection because of the undeserved general impression of video as a "frill," or a supplementary format to be added and supported only when times are good and the coffers are full. Usually the first and most important public relations and marketing campaign for the video collection takes place with the governing body.

Education of the board is well worth the time and effort it takes. Like most of the general population, board members will often think first of "movies" and "entertainment" when video collections are discussed. Some of the points that are important to make in selling a quality video collection are:

- Videocassettes are more diverse than movies; there is good solid information on many subjects to be found in this format.
- Some information is better transmitted visually than in print.
- Many people learn better through the visual than through print.
- Video offers many opportunities for learning and recreation for those whose reading skills are low.
- Film is a highly developed art form that is popular and accessible through videocassettes.
- More than 80 percent of homes in the U.S. have at least one VCR.
- Videocassettes are in the same price range as books and usually circulate at a very high rate.
- For public libraries, video serves segments of the tax-paying public who have never before used the library.

BUDGETING

With all of the demands being made on library budgets now, and with all of the new formats being introduced, what is a library to do about the allocation of resources that are not growing as quickly as the community's demands for library services?

There is no question that there are tough decisions to be made about library services and materials. But it is very short-sighted to cut the budget of a service that is growing in almost every library. A great deal of material is available on how to develop formulae for materials budget allocations. If there is interest in growing a really quality video collection, one method to use is to request a video budget allocation that reflects circulation figures. In other words, if video is 20 percent of the library's total circulation, then 20 percent of the materials budget should be spent on video.

It is my guess that if this formula were used it would almost universally result in a substantially higher video budget. While there is a paucity of good current statistical data on video service in libraries, anecdotal evidence suggests that most libraries report video circulation as 10 percent-20 percent of total materials circulation. While this is a statistic that is perhaps most relevant to public libraries, most school and academic libraries can easily demonstrate that the demand for the service would support substantial increases in budget dollars. For public libraries, perhaps the greatest trap in working with government bodies is in the charging of fees to raise revenue for the video budget. In the policy section of this chapter, we will discuss fees in greater detail, but suffice it to say, while on the surface this seems a great idea for bringing in money, it can turn a quality video collection into the corner video store, with selection criteria going out the window in the interest of building the same "pop" service that can be found all over town in said stores.

DEVELOPING A WRITTEN COLLECTION DEVELOPMENT POLICY

The most effective way the library staff can work with their governing body to guarantee a quality video collection is in the development of a written policy. As stated above, while it is important to incorporate video in an overall materials policy, there are certain considerations about video that are unique and need to be considered separately from other types of materials. The accompanying "Collection Development Policy Worksheet" can act as a blueprint for developing such a policy. The rest of this chapter will consider in detail policies needing special consideration for video collections.

POLICIES

Library policies that need to address video specifically include those concerned with formats, hardware, circulation, copyright, and access. Many of the policy considerations discussed below are controversial in some communities. Policy decisions and procedural implementation should be made in accord with the library's overall mission and philosophy.

FORMATS

The only safe bet with any audiovisual collection is that whatever formats you are using, they will be supplanted by something else. There will also be more formats introduced than will ever gain enough general acceptance to be included in a library's collection. Later in this book we will discuss some criteria for making decisions about moving into new technologies. In the meantime, what formats should be considered for a current library video collection?

VHS. The 1/2 inch VHS videocassette has been the format of choice for the general population for a number of years now. Beta, which was arguably a superior system, has virtually disappeared. Other formats are on the horizon, but for the foreseeable future, most purchases for public libraries, in particular, should be VHS.

Easy Guide for Writing a Video Collection Development Policy**

Library's mission statement

Library's demographics
- size of population/student body
- age groups served
- ethnic and racial makeup
- languages spoken
- community economic base (schools: curriculum offered)

Library's video budget
- percentage of the total library (school) budget
- comparison to video circulation percentage (schools: materials expenditures)

Video selection:
- who is responsible for selection
- what tools (reviews, etc.) will be used
- what criteria will be used

Makeup of the video collection
- fiction/nonfiction (schools: grade levels and subjects)
- adult/children
- popular/informational
- interests/needs of population
- special collections

Video collection organization
- cataloging and classification to be used
- access through main library catalog
- collection location (separate or interfiled?)

Policies
- which formats are offered
- circulation
  - length of loan period
  - how many may be borrowed
  - late, lost, damaged fees
  - interlibrary loan
- access
  - adoption of Freedom To View statement
  - access by minors
  - reconsideration of challenged materials
- collection evaluation
  - stated evaluation process
  - deaccession policies

** Ideally this will be incorporated in the library's overall collection development policy.

As more than 80 percent of the homes in the U.S. have a VHS videocassette player, this only makes sense.

Laserdiscs. There is no question that for those who care about film, laserdisc resolution is far superior to tape. Additionally, laserdiscs offer features not available on VHS, such as random access, which makes it very valuable for teaching situations. Additional soundtracks with director commentary, additional scenes cut from the theatrical release, and state-of-the-art sound reproduction make laserdiscs the best way to reproduce films.

The question about laserdiscs and the library collection is in their potential for use. For a school or academic institution, the decision can be made on the basis of availability of equipment and faculty trained to use it (use of random access capability, particularly). For a public library the decision is more problematic. This is a case where a user survey can be very helpful. How many people in the community have access to laserdisc players? How many are interested in borrowing laserdiscs from the library? What types of programs would they like the library to carry (feature films, operas, etc.)?

CD-ROMS. There is no question that CD-ROM is the hot new format. With most new personal computers now coming loaded with a CD-ROM drive, and the bundling of encyclopedias and games with the computer purchase, there is a sudden upsurge in CD-ROM demand. CD-ROMs have already proven themselves crucial in library reference collections. But what is their role *vis a vis* the video collection?

Much has been made of the capability to combine print, sound, and motion pictures on CD-ROM. While many programs are still clunky and of mediocre quality, there are some that are simply dazzling. But even the best, at this point, have moving images that are reminiscent of hand-cranked movie projectors. At this point, decisions about adding CD-ROM should be based on their usefulness as reference material and entertainment (such as games). CD-ROM is not yet a good format for viewing motion pictures.

Other new formats on the horizon, such as the promising digital videodisc, must be evaluated as they emerge. The rule of thumb here is that *no* format, no matter how sophisticated, exciting, or even useful, is practical unless it can be utilized by the intended users. In the school and academic setting this means having the resources to purchase appropriate equipment and train instructors. In the public library this means having a large enough population with access to equipment to make purchases economically feasible.

HARDWARE

The amount and type of equipment needed is a major question for any audiovisual department in any library. In the school or academic setting it is assumed that sufficient equipment must be purchased for whatever formats are offered. The public library does not have this same obligation. So what equipment is appropriate for a public library to provide for use with a VHS videocassette collection?

There are three considerations when purchasing equipment for the public library. First, every video collection needs at least one VCR for purposes of previewing and checking cassettes for condition and damage. This can be any videocassette player, unless there will be heavy use, in which case an industrial model is needed.

Second is equipment for in-house programming. If the library does extensive public programming of videos, and has an auditorium, a stationary video projection system is probably called for. This allows for large screen projection to a sizable audience. There are both regular projection (as in movie projection from the back of the room) and rear-screen, which is a large screen with the projection coming from behind the screen.

If the library needs to transport equipment from department to department, then a rolling cart with the equipment is a good idea. This prevents wear and tear, and allows the connections between VCR and monitor, for example, to stay in place. In addition to the traditional VCR and monitor configuration, there are now some very good portable video projectors on the market.

In any case, when purchasing for this type of use, it is a good idea to spend the extra money to acquire institutional type equipment, such as that used in schools. There are audiovisual equipment dealers who specialize in this type of equipment, and they can be helpful in assessing the library's needs and in making suggestions. The local school district can probably make a recommendation.

The third type of equipment to consider is for in-house viewing via carrel. With video becoming more and more important as a research tool, a library serving any kind of research function will want to consider making this service available. Another reason for a library to consider carrel viewing is a situation (such as an urban business center) where people come to spend time on lunch hours, etc. And, a very important reason is to provide access to videos for people who do not otherwise have access to a VCR. Important considerations in providing this service is whether the screenings are controlled by the viewer from the carrel, or by staff in a central location. And, with any library programming function (including carrel viewing) the copyright laws must be considered. These will be treated in detail later in this chapter.

Lastly, a library may want to purchase inspection machinery. It was widely believed that one of the advantages of moving from 16mm film to videocassettes was that the expensive and time-consuming film inspection process could be eliminated. While this is mostly true, videocassettes have proved to be less indestructible than we had all hoped. It is true that because of the low price of much video these days, replacement is far more economical than repair. However, it is also true that periodic checking and cleaning through a machine does extend the life of the collection and insure its visual quality. Also, libraries with a substantial number of expensive and specialized programs will want to extend their life. Inspection machinery varies widely in price, and should be evaluated based on the size and circulation of the video collection. Audiovisual equipment dealers can make recommendations.

CIRCULATION POLICIES

Perhaps in no other aspect of library practice has video been treated as differently from other library's materials as it has in circulation policies. There are two reasons for this. First, as video replaced 16mm films in many libraries, the practice of loaning materials overnight was passed on to the video collection. The second was the use of the video store model for the library video collection. This, too, called for overnight or two-day circulation.

As video collections become larger, and videos become more integrated into the mainstream of library service, it is a good idea to review these policies. Perhaps the best advice about policies is this: Keep It Simple. The closer the policies for video (and all other materials) are to the basic book borrowing policies, the better they will serve both borrowers and the easier they will be to administer for the staff. Reducing special procedures also makes good fiscal sense.

Circulation Systems and Procedures. Much of the following section applies specifically to public libraries, as by definition many school and academic media centers operate as totally separate entities from the institution's library, and loans for classroom use call for a different system than public circulation. Some libraries go through a long and arduous process to select and install a separate circulation system for the video department. Some of this is due, of course, to existing systems that were installed long enough ago that video does not easily fit. Yet, if video were treated exactly like books a great deal of this trouble and expense could be avoided.

Length of Loan. Is there good reason to continue to circulate all video on an overnight basis? This is a question that each library should ask in a thorough policy review. In the early days of video collections it was true that libraries literally couldn't keep the videos on the shelf. Often there were only a handful of titles in at any time. Longer circulation periods would have made this difficult situation even worse. But now that video collections have grown in size and have matured, is there good reason to continue to keep loan periods short?

This is a question that is of particular relevance to the nonfiction video collection. While the latest Arnold Schwarzenegger flick may go out several times in a week when it is new, demand even for it will disappear after awhile. Meanwhile, a how-to or documentary program may call for more time. The classic case is the "21 Days to Quitting Smoking" tape, which many libraries had on overnight loan. As video is being used for more purposes than an hour's entertainment, it is worth considering extending the loan period. And borrowers very much appreciate the luxury of not having to run back to the library again in twenty-four hours. Perhaps the library might consider policies close to the book collection, with selected "best sellers" circulating for a short period, and all others for a longer period of time. The closer this can come to the book circulation policies, the better for everyone.

Age Restrictions. While we will treat the whole issue of age later in the section on access, it also needs to be mentioned in the circulation discussion. Intellectual freedom issues aside, the same rule applies here as for policies about length of loan. If there are circulation restrictions on age, has this been considered on any basis except the perceived need to comply with movie ratings? Do these policies match those for the book collection?

As has been mentioned before, often policies for the video collection grew out of policies for the 16mm film collection. In that case there really was some justification for age restrictions on borrowing. Film was a very expensive medium, with feature length films sometimes costing close to $1,000, with the shortest children's story in the $200 range. Film was also very fragile, and it took equipment that was both expensive and complicated to show it.

Beyond the concern for films getting damaged in use was the daunting financial responsibility of film borrowing. I do not know of a case anywhere where children were given free access to borrow from a film collection, notwithstanding the cadre of sixth graders who proudly and responsibly ran the projectors at school.

In the early days of video collections, financial responsibility was again an issue as far as circulation to children was concerned, though more libraries moved to make the materials available. But with the economics of video having changed so completely this is no longer a viable argument against open access.

Ease of use of the video equipment (most two-year-olds can operate a VCR) and inexpensive videocassettes make it possible, and even preferable, to make video available to children for borrowing. This is true both for the public library and for the school library, where "homework videos" have enjoyed success in many school media centers. This collection usually contains good educational programs on curriculum subjects which students may use for research purposes.

In public libraries the ideal is certainly having open access to video circulation to all borrowers. The fact of the matter is that in some communities librarians feel community perceptions about "movies" and their content may make this a very volatile issue. Where this is the case consideration can be given to creating a collection of age-appropriate video programs in the children's section of the library. (See the Appendix for "Access for Children and Young People to Videotapes and Other Nonprint Formats: An Interpretation of the Library Bill of Rights.")

Lost and Late Fees. Once again, policies relating to lost, damaged, and late videos should reflect the library's policies for other materials. In collections with highly popular recent movies, it has been tempting to impose very high late fees in order to encourage prompt return by borrowers. This is always more of a problem with materials that can only be kept for a short period of time. As collections have evolved and matured, many libraries charge in the range of $1 per day for overdue videos, but this varies with the library. In setting these fees, it is important to balance the desire to motivate prompt return with concern for intimidating borrowers with high fees.

Fees charged for replacing lost or damaged cassettes is another variable. As with books, the replacement cost for a video can vary widely. Some libraries charge actual cost of the individual video, while others charge a set fee (around $25) for any lost or damaged tape. Those using the second method have discovered that this usually evens out between the titles the library was able to obtain at a below-retail cost with those (very often the best children's material) which are considerably more expensive.

Borrowing Fees. How tempting it is to set up a highly popular collection like feature film videocassettes, make them circulate overnight, and charge a fee. It is without a doubt a surefire way to provide a service and make money at the same time. But is it worth the downside?

There are several problems with the concept of charging fees.

First, and there is certainly a great deal of controversy about this in the profession, the library is charging taxpayers twice. If these videos are purchased with public funds, does it not follow that they are public property?

The second problem with fees is that they can drive and even destroy a collection development policy. If bringing in money through the collection is a goal, then selecting only the best-known, most popular and most mainstream programs becomes very tempting. It makes the library just another video store, and, understandably causes friction with local video store owners. While the furor of a few years ago in which video store owners were accusing libraries of unfair competition has largely died down, there is a point to be made that the library collection shouldn't mirror the video store.

Another reason not to separate video out as a self-supporting service is that it says that this collection is not central to the library's mission. If extra money is collected for the service we are saying that it is a "frill," rather than the important source of information and enlightenment that it should be. It also puts the collection out of the realm of those who use the library because of economic need.

There is no doubt that the library must make more and more difficult choices about collections as new formats are introduced and funds may shrink. But each service needs to be considered for its contribution to the whole collection, and collections are developed around the information needed by the community and provided by the material, not by whether that material is transmitted via print, moving image, or sound. (See the Appendix for the *Library Bill of Rights* Interpretation "Economic Barriers to Information.")

Interlibrary Loan. In early days of library video collections there were tales of videos disappearing during transport from one library to another. One issue that cannot be debated is that video has a higher "street value" than any other format. But interlibrary loan really isn't about sharing Sylvester Stallone. As video collections mature and libraries begin to build specialized collections, interlibrary loan should be a part of the service, as it is with other types of library material. This is an issue which has caused major debates, and the American Library Association is currently struggling with recommendations. It is also an issue with particular importance for academic libraries, as much of the material that is specialized and hard to find is in academic libraries. Researchers need to be able to access material no matter what its location.

While we have talked a great deal about video not being any

more expensive than books, there are, of course, videos with price tags similar to reference books. Because of copyright restrictions, it is not just a matter of making a copy of a tape and sending it on to someone who needs it. Some libraries are reluctant to make these materials available, especially if they are rare or "one of a kind."

Once more this is an issue of treating video the same as the book collection. Interlibrary loan policies should apply to all library materials equally. Eventually it will be possible to transmit moving images easily via computer, and once copyright laws are worked out (a monumental task in and of itself) the actual physical moving of material will be immaterial. This, however, is a long way off for most libraries. In the meantime, it is important to make essential material available to those who need it, regardless of proximity.

COPYRIGHT

While the preposterous (though true) tales from the late 1980s of retired FBI agents going to public libraries pretending to be Boy Scout leaders and trying to entrap librarians into loaning them movies in violation of the public performance section of the copyright law have mercifully faded, the ambiguous, frustrating video copyright laws have probably caused librarians more headaches than any other aspect of library service over the last ten years.

A disclaimer: What follows is not legal advice. It is meant to highlight and clarify the parts of the current copyright regulations as they relate to video collections in libraries, and to give general guidelines on how to stay within the law with minimum fuss and frustration. As far as legal advice is concerned, it is very good practice for the person in charge of the library's video collection to supply the library's legal counsel with current information about libraries, video, and the copyright law (see the bibliography for suggestions). Intellectual property law is a complex specialty in the legal profession, and most library attorneys do not have extensive background in this area. Having said that, how does one make sense of these confusing regulations, and how does the library deal with this area without an undue expenditure of time and legal fees?

The current copyright law was passed by Congress in 1976, and went into effect in 1978. In that statement is the genesis of the confusion over libraries and videocassette collections. In 1976 no one foresaw the home video revolution. Therefore, home video had to try to fit in to regulations that were written from a different perspective.

As with many complex sets of regulations, the best efforts of all involved (to put the best interpretation on special interests vs. public interests) still left large areas of ambiguity and confusion. In this discussion we will focus on the areas that most often impact libraries and video collections: *fair use*, *public performance*, and *the face-to-face teaching exemption*. We will also briefly discuss *off-air taping* and *ethics and the copyright law*.

Section 106 of the copyright law spells out very clearly what are the basic rights of the videocassette copyright holder. These are:

1. to reproduce the copyrighted work in copies;
2. to prepare derivative works based upon the copyrighted work;
3. to distribute copies of the copyrighted work to the public by sale or other transfer of ownership, or by rental, lease, or lending;
4. in the case of motion pictures, to perform the copyrighted work publicly; and
5. in the case of motion pictures, to display the copyrighted work publicly.

What does all this mean to libraries? Before considering these five rights, it is important to understand the concept of "copyright holder." Very often (almost always in the case of feature films) the copyright holder is not the company from which you purchase a copy of the tape. Usually, the producer of the program owns the copyright, and assigns the rights to sell it to various distributors. The rights are usually divided between a number of specialists for selling to the consumer market; to the education market; to television; to foreign markets, etc. But the right to assign distribution *always* remains with the copyright owner. In other words, Baker & Taylor and Ingram do not own the copyrights for the tapes you purchase from them.

What the first right means to libraries is that it is not permissible to purchase a copy of a cassette and then make a copy of it to circulate. Libraries have sometimes felt that an expensive tape is too precious just to send out, since it might be ruined right away. As long as there is a distributor available for a program, a library may not "protect" its collection by copying. The owner of the copyright controls all legal copies made. They may control the copies themselves, or assign this to a licensed distributor.

The second right, "preparation of derivative works" means that a tape may not be tampered with by a purchaser and then used. In school collections this often takes the form of teachers pulling segments out of various programs and putting them together to make a teaching tool. This might enhance effective teaching, but it is illegal. This right also makes it illegal to decide that a film is really good except for some violent or sexy scenes and then edit the tape. Only the copyright owner has the right to make a decision about what should or should not be included in a program. The decision to purchase or not purchase a program has to be made based on what is there.

The third right has sometimes been confusing for libraries as well as producers and distributors. It is easy to read this as meaning that the copyright owner has the right to say that libraries are not allowed to loan tapes after they have been purchased. This is not the case. Because of something called the "first sale doctrine," once a legal copy has been purchased, that copy can be re-sold, circulated or rented, as long as other parts of the law (public performance, fair use) are not violated.

The last two rights deal directly with public performance and will be discussed in detail below. Without question, this is the part of the law that has caused the most headaches for libraries and copyright owners alike.

The Public Performance Dilemma. What constitutes a public performance? This seemingly simple question continues to plague both copyright owners and video users of all types. To complicate matters even more, the implications of the public performance issue are different for different types of libraries. I detail these implications for each type of library as clearly and simply as possible below.

The crux of the debate has been this—the copyright owners (represented by the MPAA in the case of feature films) have maintained that a library is a public place, therefore any viewing of a video in that place is a public performance. This includes both viewing by individuals in carrels, and screenings (even for one person) in any room in the library. Many librarians have contended that one or two people viewing a video in a carrel or room in the library falls under the provisions of fair use (fair use will be discussed in detail later). There are areas where all parties involved agree. For example, it is undisputed that a library's public program, such as a travel series or story hour, falls under the category of a public performance, and that a license is necessary.

How does this situation differ for different types of libraries? For a public library, the issue really revolves around whether or not carrels are used for screening videos in the library. While the library may interpret the law to mean that one or two people in a carrel do not constitute a public performance, librarians need to be aware that many copyright owners do not see this in the same way. Another problem for public libraries is in the area of loaning videos to groups. While everyone agrees that an individual may borrow and screen a video at home for family and a few friends, an organized community group may not screen a video without a public performance license. In other words, youth groups, churches, senior centers, etc., must use only public performance videos for programs.

For academic libraries, the problem also revolves around carrels. For example, videos put on reserve by a professor for viewing by students in a class must have public performance licenses if the law is interpreted narrowly. There are questions for school libraries, as well. In the strictest interpretation, a student missing a class in which a video was used may not view it later in a carrel in the school library, as this would be a public performance.

So what is a library to do? What is the librarian's responsibility?

First, all videos are not equal as far as public performance licenses are concerned. It is true that most home video (feature films, popular how-tos, etc.) are released as "home use only," and licenses must be obtained for them to be used for public programs. On the other hand, most educational materials (from traditional educational film distributors), as well as much independent and alternative video, come with public performance rights. While the initial price for some of these programs may be higher, you do often get more for your money. Some companies will also offer public performance rights on "home-use only" videos for an extra fee.

If the library offers extensive public programming of feature film videos, it is also possible to purchase blanket licenses for portions of the feature film video collection. The two companies offering licenses (for movies from different studios) are: Public Media, Inc., 5547 N. Ravenswood, Chicago, IL 60640; (800) 826-3456; and Motion Picture Licensing Corporation, 13315 Washington Blvd., Los Angeles, CA 90066; (800) 426-8855. A warning, however: these blanket licenses are for library buildings *only*; they do not cover community groups borrowing them for use. It is tempting to disregard what appears to be huge, rich movie studios worrying about economic harm from a small library showing *Jurassic Park* to a few children on a summer afternoon. But the law also protects those small, independent, and alternative filmmakers whose work needs to be compensated fairly.

Unlike public libraries, schools do have some flexibility with home-use only videos. After the copyright law was passed in 1976, teachers all around the country protested the fact that they could no longer use feature films in their teaching if they followed the letter of the law. The House Subcommittee on Copyright agreed to take up the matter and Congress passed Section 110.1, known as the "face-to-face teaching exemption." It is very narrow in focus, as the copyright owners were reluctant to open the law too far. Basically, the exemption permits the use of home-use only videocassettes in classrooms under these strict circumstances.

— The performance must be by instructors (including guest lecturers) or by pupils; and
— the performance is in connection with face-to-face teaching activities; and
— the entire audience is involved in the teaching activity; and
— the entire audience is in the same room or same general area; and
— the teaching activities are conducted by a non-profit education institution; and
— the performance takes place in a classroom or similar place devoted to instruction, such as a school library, gym, auditorium, or workshop; and
— the videotape is lawfully made; the person responsible had no reason to believe that the videotape was unlawfully made.[3]

In a nutshell, an English instructor teaching a unit on Shakespeare could show Zeffirelli's *Romeo and Juliet* as a part of the lesson. The teacher could not reward the class for being attentive during the rest of the week by showing *Ace Ventura, Pet Detective* on Friday afternoon. And the tape used needs to be from the library or video store, not a personal copy taped off cable a couple of years ago. (More about off-air taping below.)

What is the librarian's responsibility? A few years ago the Motion Picture Association of America suggested that librarians had the responsibility to question those borrowing videos to be sure that a public performance was not in the offing, and that the librarians bore the responsibility to police the use of the videos in the collection. There are two problems with this.

First, it directly violates professional ethics. Librarians do not cross examine borrowers about the intended use of library materials of any kind. There is a middle ground. I am among those who agree that the library does bear a certain responsibility to inform users about the public performance law. One way to do this in any type of library is to provide users a written notice about public performance regulations. This can either be given to borrowers as they are registering to use the library, or can be a brochure made available in the part of the library where videos are displayed, or at the check-out desk. For any library loaning to teachers, the face-to-face teaching exemption should also be included in any explanation of the public performance law.

The other problem for librarians is keeping track of which videos have public performance rights and which do not. This issue can be complicated by the fact that some video distributors in the consumer business do not understand the concept. If a library is going to use tapes for library programs, or to loan to community groups for programming, this should be made clear, and should be negotiated and expressed in writing when purchasing. This is not as complicated as it seems, as single-source distributors (much educational material) includes the rights, and most feature films and consumer how-tos do not. Major library suppliers now sell labels that can be affixed to a tape to indicate that it may be used for public performance. A library may even have the situation of having two copies of a tape, one with public performance rights and one without. An example of this might be certain performance videos (operas, ballets) available from Home Vision, which offers a public performance license to its programs for an extra fee. An additional point about labeling—when affixing labels and notices to tapes purchased for the library, be sure that the official copyright notice on the tape is not obscured.

Fair Use. After all the discussion of what does and does not constitute public performance, and how this affects different libraries, it must also be said that there are some provisions for educational use of video in the copyright law. These are found in the section on "fair use," and do cover many of the uses made of video for research and reference.

Basically, the fair use provisions state that a video may be used for criticism, comment, news reporting, teaching, scholarship, or research. In so doing the following factors must be considered:

— the purpose and character of the use, including whether such use is of a commercial nature or is for nonprofit educational purposes;
— the nature of the copyrighted work;
— the amount and substantiality of the portion used in relation to the copyrighted work as a whole; and
— the effect of the use upon the potential market for or value of the copyrighted work.

Some examples of how this works for libraries might be a user in a public library who wants to show videos for their children and would like to look at parts of several to choose the most appropriate; or a student doing a research project on earthquakes looking at several videos about weather to find appropriate material. A travel lecturer might show one scene from a video to illustrate a lecture point. On the other hand, copying of the videos is not permitted, except when a license has been purchased from the appropriate distribution source. A librarian, with seemingly good intentions, once told me her library wanted to make a copy of a particularly expensive tape, because they wanted to do a continuous screening of the program, which had public performance rights attached, for a community event and didn't want to wear out the original. As with so much connected to copyright, it is easy to be so focused on what is good for library users, the rights of the artists who made the program to be fairly compensated for their work is forgotten.

Off-Air Taping. The first advice I can give to *public* libraries about off-air taping is that unless you have a professional audiovisual department with professional technicians, don't do it. In almost all instances, it is better to purchase professionally manufactured tapes, both for circulation and for programming. It is, indeed, possible to physically tape off the air, and it is possible in many cases to purchase the rights to do so, but the question is whether or not it is a good idea. Quality control is almost always a problem with amateur copying.

Academic institutions are another matter altogether. In many cases there are facilities and staff to handle off-air taping skillfully and legally. As with other parts of the copyright law, however, there are confusing and very strict regulations. Again, as with the face-to-face teaching exemption (see above), this part of the law was developed through the offices of the congressional subcommittee on copyright after the new law was passed by Congress.

Very specifically, what the off-air taping guidelines allow is this:

— programs may be taped during transmission by non-profit educational institutions and kept forty-five days, then erased;
— taping may take place at home, but all other restrictions apply;
— programs may be shown once and repeated for reinforcement once in the first ten school days within the forty-five day period—after that may they only be shown for teacher evaluation;
— schools can only tape at a specific teacher request—they can't anticipate requests—teachers may only request a specific program once;
— limited copies may be made to fill requests;
— educators can't alter the program (but may use a portion) and portions can't be part of an anthology;
— all copies must display the copyright notice; and
— educational institutions are expected to enforce these regulations.

Fortunately, most school districts and academic institutions have developed policies and procedures and forms for offering off-air taping. If policies are needed, I highly recommend Charles Vleck's *Copyright Policy Development: A Resource Book for Educators* (Copyright Information Services, 1988).

Another caution to schools and academic institutions in particular is that there are also restrictions on closed-circuit broadcast of videotapes. Again, licenses are needed and can usually be worked out with the program's educational distributor. Just because broadcast is only within an institution does not mean that it is considered a "single user."

All that having been said, there are some programs that can be taped off the air under the fair use provisions. Television newscasts are considered to be in the public domain, and can be taped and used. A big caution here, though. This applies only to newscasts, not to news "magazines." In other words, it is permissible to tape and use the CBS Evening News. It is not permissible to tape and use *60 Minutes* except under the off-air taping guidelines. C-Span allows unrestricted taping and use by educational institutions.

Ethics and the Copyright Law. In addition to the problems posed by these legal ambiguities, the copyright law as it stands today can also challenge the librarian with ethical considerations. While much of the furor of the late 1980s over libraries loaning home video has now died down, there are some questions which have never been satisfactorily resolved.

The most troubling, without doubt, is the question of the showing of videos in carrels in libraries. While many in the library profession believe that the library's right to do so would be upheld by the courts (and more and more attorneys agree), the fact is that no test case has yet emerged. Libraries should interpret this portion of the law not through ignorance, but with policies considered, established, and agreed on by staff, governing body, and library legal counsel.

The same is true of how the library chooses to deal with the notification of library users about the legal use of videos (and equipment, for that matter.) Most in the profession would agree, I think, that the librarian's first responsibility is to protect the privacy of the library user. Asking about intended use of materials being borrowed is not appropriate. Yet, in order to also uphold the law of the land, no matter how ambiguous, it behooves the library to notify users in some way about the legalities of using "home use only" videotapes.

For better or worse, these are the regulations we are expected to cope with. For a long time there was a strong movement urging all parties to come to some sort of agreement that would make regulations clearer for everyone. Reaching accord on this particular set of regulations has become moot with the explosion of the communications technologies. Electronic publishing, both print and image, presents a labyrinth of intellectual property issues. It is increasingly clear that an entirely new set of copyright regulations need to be established, and that all of the old rules will not apply. In the meantime, librarians will just have to muddle along doing the best we can to balance the sometimes opposing interests of users and producers.

ACCESS

It is an interesting exercise to ponder what would happen if the next time a delivery of new books was opened the librarian was greeted with book jackets with letters on each indicating who should not be allowed to read the book in question. The resulting cries of outrage would be heard from coast to coast. Yet this is precisely what happens every time the library gets a delivery of feature film videos. What's more, many library users object vociferously if these letters do not appear on *all* videos. In any discussion of access to the library video collection, it is useful to look at what those MPAA ratings are all about, and what the library's responsibility is vis a vis the ratings system.

MPAA Ratings. The key point in any discussion of the ratings system is that they are *guidelines*, and do not have the force of law. Some states, it is true, have passed laws relating to the ratings and video stores, and these will be discussed a little later. In the meantime, some background on the ratings system.

Objecting to movie content didn't start in the 1960s with the sexual revolution. In earlier decades the dreaded Hayes Office imposed official censorship on movies, leading to such familiar absurdities as the "twin bed syndrome," in which even married couples could not be seen in bed together. By the 1960s, however, these restrictions had disappeared, and suddenly, "anything goes" was the motto of many filmmakers. Like most arts, film reflected what was happening in the society at large. The outrage expressed by some segments of the population was actually eerily similar to what is happening currently with the controversy over violence and sex on television and in video games. Members of Congress began making noises about legislation to restrict what could be portrayed on movie screens.

As so often happens, the solution (voluntary ratings which many industry officials didn't agree with) was actually what appeared to be the best compromise at the time. There seemed little doubt that there would be official censorship if something wasn't done.

Thus the movie industry undertook "self-policing" through a set of letters that would appear on movies and in ads, so that parents could be guided in "appropriateness" for their children's viewing. In the beginning there were fewer ratings than we have today—G (general audience), PG (parental guidance suggested), R (restricted to anyone under 17 without a parent or guardian in attendance), and X (no one under 18 admitted under any circumstances). Newspapers followed suit, refusing advertising for X-rated films—the kiss of death for profit-conscious movie studios.

What is absolutely true, but not always apparent to the public at large, is that the ratings system was never designed to replace the selection process of library professionals building an appropriate collection for a specific user population. The ratings are actually assigned by a committee of people, a group of parents who allegedly represent a cross-section of the American population, whose identities are carefully guarded.

In the time since the establishment of those initial ratings, more have been added. PG-13 was a new rating that came about when Spielberg's *Indiana Jones and the Temple of Doom* was released, because it was deemed too intense, and was in danger of receiving an "R" rating, thus eliminating its largest audience—teenagers. Then, more recently, the "NC-17" rating was established to deal with serious adult films that went beyond the "acceptable limits" of the "R" rating. The film in question was *Henry and June*, the story of Henry Miller, his wife, and his mistress. While the filmmakers felt the eroticism that would get the "X" rating was necessary, it was also important to be able to advertise a film that critics agreed was a fine work of art.

It is important for librarians to remember a couple of key points—first, these ratings were established for the guidance of theater owners and parents, and second, they do not have the force of law. Somehow, the Motion Picture Association of America (the trade association for the movie business) has skillfully promoted this program until it has taken on the aura of motherhood, the flag and apple pie.

Film producers voluntarily submit films to this MPAA committee for evaluation and the assignment of a rating. The committee determines the rating by the evaluation of language, sexual situations, and violence. If the filmmaker doesn't want to accept the rating, the film can be re-edited and then re-submitted. In an attempt to avoid "censorship" the committee doesn't tell the filmmaker what to cut, so it can become something of a guessing game.

As with any such system, much is arbitrary. Much is also cynical. The appearance of an "R" rating makes a film more appealing to the lucrative young audience, and filmmakers have been known to deliberately go for an "R" by adding sex and violence. It works the same way at the other end of the ratings, too. There is the tale of a monumentally successful film that had an extra scene shot to add a mild obscenity to keep from getting the dreaded "G" rating. It is conventional wisdom that *nobody* wants to see a "G" picture.

When the video rental business began, the ratings were transferred from just the film to the video boxes, as well. Thus, librarians became unwitting participants in the system. At one point, some libraries made the decision to remove or obscure the labels on the boxes. This met with objections from two sources—one was parents who have learned to depend on these arbitrary guides for their family's viewing; and the other was the American Library Association, pointing out that it was not the practice of librarians to remove anything from library materials. In many cases, though we may disagree with the system itself, the ratings can be of assistance to busy librarians. (See the Appendix for "Statement on Labeling: An Interpretation of the Library Bill of Rights.")

Minors and the Video Collection. It would be naïve to suggest that the video collection does not have the potential for censorship problems, particularly around "R" rated videos and children. Yet, it has been a pleasant surprise that most libraries report user complaints about videos have been no more common than for book collections.

The Library Bill of Rights protects the rights of children to equal access to library materials. In 1989 the American Library Association Council passed "Access for Children and Young People to Videotapes and Other Nonprint Formats: An Interpretation of the Library Bill of Rights." In part that statement says, "The 'right to use a library' includes use of, and access to all library materials and services. Thus, practices which allow adults to use some services and materials which are denied to minors abridge use based on age.

...It is the parents—and only parents—who may restrict their children—and only their children—from access to library materials and services. People who would rather their children did not have access to certain materials should so advise their children. The library and its staff are responsible for providing equal access to library materials and services for all library users." (A copy of the full text of this document appears in the appendix.)

There are some ways libraries can assist parents with their responsibility for monitoring their own children's video borrowing and viewing. One is to prominently display helpful movie guides near the video collection. In addition to those guides mentioned earlier in this text, there are some specifically aimed at "family viewing." Another help to parents is for a collection of quality children's videos to be placed in the children's department. This has proved to be a very popular service in many libraries.

Some type of notification, expressed in a positive manner, can also be helpful. I particularly like this wording from the Santa Monica Public Library in California, which appears in a brochure for video collection users, "The library is not responsible for audience suitability. Please preview to avoid misunderstandings."

As was mentioned earlier, there are some states that now have laws on the books prohibiting the loaning of "R" rated videos to minors, among other restrictions. In several states where there is such a law, libraries were specifically excluded. It is a good idea to find out what the law is in your state, and to be sure that library staff and legal counsel have a clear understanding of the library's legal stance.

Reconsideration of Challenged Materials. In an interview a couple of years ago, author Nat Hentoff said it best, " . . . censorship remains the strongest drive in human nature, with sex a weak second."[4]

While it is true that the cases of attempted video censorship have not been any more frequent than those for books, it is still important to have *written* policies and procedures, and to train all staff in how to handle these situations. This is a case in which the procedures can follow those of the book collection. In fact, this is a very good idea, in that it puts all library materials on an equal footing.

As with any objection to materials in the library, there are certain procedures that should be followed. One is to treat the complaint seriously; another is to ask the person to express the complaint in writing; and a third is to make sure a response is forthcoming from the proper source at the library. All of this is made easier for everyone if there is a clear policy in place, and *all* staff members working with the public are familiar with the procedures to follow. While much of this seems obvious, anyone who has had to face an angry member of the public knows it is a stressful experience. A librarian I know, who has more than thirty years experience in film and video told me that the last time he was faced with the situation his "hands shook" and he felt his "face turning hot and red." It is at this time when set procedures come to the rescue.

ALA's Office for Intellectual Freedom can be very helpful in providing materials to assist the library in establishing a written form. They will provide a document, "Dealing with Concerns About Library Resources" (ISBN 8389-6487-7) that provides both tips and an actual form that can be adapted for library use in handling complaints. Its main points include the following.

— Maintain a materials selection policy.
— Maintain a library service policy.
— Maintain a clearly defined method for handling complaints.
— Maintain in-service training.
— Maintain lines of communication with civic, religious, educational, and political bodies of the community.
— Maintain a vigorous public information program on behalf of intellectual freedom.
— Maintain familiarity with any local municipal and state legislation pertaining to intellectual freedom and First Amendment rights.

Again, it would be naïve to suggest that the video collection does not carry built-in possibilities for the censor. Images are very powerful. It would be wrong of me to make this argument while promoting the importance of motion pictures, and then duck the issue here. Yet, a carefully selected collection, built for the library's constituency, with the back-up of solid policies and procedures, will minimize problems. And, it is also true that in any department, objections are often from unexpected sources about unexpected materials, such as the objection to the Disney version of *Peter Pan* on the basis that it promotes the occult.

One more aid the library governing body might want to adopt, along with the Library Bill of Rights, is the Freedom To View statement. This short and effective tool was developed by the American Film and Video Association, a professional organization of librarians, educators, and filmmakers, precisely for assisting libraries and schools. It appears in its entirety in the box on page 71.

Freedom to View

The FREEDOM TO VIEW, along with the freedom to speak, to hear, and to read, is protected by the First Amendment to the Constitution of the United States. In a free society, there is no place for censorship of any medium of expression. Therefore these principles are affirmed:

1. To provide the broadest access to film, video, and other audiovisual materials because they are a means for the communication of ideas. Liberty of circulation is essential to insure the constitutional guarantees of freedom of expression.
2. To protect the confidentiality of all individuals and institutions using film, video, and other audiovisual materials.
3. To provide film, video, and other audiovisual materials which represent a diversity of views and expression. Selection of a work does not constitute or imply agreement with or approval of the content.
4. To provide a diversity of viewpoints without the constraint of labeling or prejudging film, video, or other audiovisual materials on the basis of the moral, religious, or political beliefs of the producer or filmmaker or on the basis of controversial content.
5. To contest vigorously, by all lawful means, every encroachment upon the public's freedom to view.

This statement was originally drafted by the Freedom to View Committee of the American Film and Video Association (formerly the Educational Film Library Association) and was adopted by the AFVA Board of Directors in February 1979. This statement was updated and approved by the AFVA Board of Directors in 1989.

BIBLIOGRAPHY

Collection Development

Audiovisual Policies in ARL Libraries: SPEC Kit no. 162. Washington, DC, Association of Research Libraries, 1990.

Brancolini, Kristine, ed. *Audiovisual Policies in College Libraries: Clip Note #14.* Chicago, Association of College and Research Libraries, 1991.

Ellison, John. *Media Librarianship.* New York, Neal-Schuman, 1985.

Handman, Gary. *Video Collection Development in Multi-Type Libraries: A Handbook.* Westport, CT, Greenwood Press, 1994.

Hedges, Michael. "Managing an Integrated Video Collection." *Wilson Library Bulletin* 67:10, June 1993, pp. 32–35.

Kaye, Allen L. *Video and Other Nonprint Resources in the Small Library.* Chicago, ALA, 1991.

Mason, Sally. "Video Verite: Creating a Successful Library Video Service." *Library Journal* 117:19, November 15, 1992, pp. 32–36.

Scholtz, James. *Developing and Maintaining Video Collections in Libraries.* Santa Barbara, CA, ABC-Clio, 1988.

Scholtz, James. *Library Video Policies and Procedures for Libraries*. Santa Barbara, CA, ABC-Clio, 1991.

Slyhoff, Merle. "The Video Librarian's Hide and Seek: Videotapes and Collection Development." *Wilson Library Bulletin* 67:10, June 1993, pp. 36–38.

Copyright

Galvin, Thomas and Sally Mason, eds. "Video, Libraries and the Law: Finding the Balance." *American Libraries* 20:2, February 1989, pp. 110–119.

Heller, James S. "The Public Performance Right in Libraries: Is There Anything Fair About It?" *Law Library Journal* 84:2, Spring 1992, pp.315–340.

Keelan, Mary. "Circulating Media in Public Libraries: What Is Legal? What Is Safe?" *The Bookmark* (50:2), Winter 1992, pp. 1–5.

Kreamer, Jean T., Raymond Morgan Allen, and Thomas L. Kreamer. "Video and Copyright: An Overview of Some Basic Issues." *Sightlines*, Fall 1989.

Miller, Jerome K. *Using Copyrighted Videocassettes in Classrooms, Libraries, and Training Centers*. Friday Harbor, WA, Copyright Information Service, 1988.

Reed, Mary Hutchings. *Copyright Primer for Librarians and Educators*. Chicago, ALA, 1987.

———— and Debra Stanek. "Library and Classroom Use of Copyrighted Videotapes and Computer Software." *American Libraries*, February 1986.

Valauskas, Edward J. "Copyright: Know Your Electronic Rights!" *Library Journal*, August 1992, pp. 40–43.

Vleck, Charles W. *Copyright Policy Development: A Resource Book for Educators*. Friday Harbor, WA, Copyright Information Service, 1987.

Access

Beck, Susan. "Videos and Minors: Open Questions." *School Library Journal*, June 1988, pp. 45–46.

Crist, Judith, Gordon Conable, and Sally Mason. "Freedom to View, Instinct to Censor," *Newsletter on Intellectual Freedom*, September 1989.

McIntyre, Ron. "Video and Access for Minors." *Sightlines*, Winter 1990, pp. 37–41.

Mason, Sally. "Access to Video by Minors: It's Only Right." *Journal of Youth Services in Libraries*, Fall 1990.

Pitman, Randy. "We Are the Censors" (Parts 1 and 2). *Video Librarian* 7:4/5, June, 1992; July-August 1992.

5 VIDEO COLLECTION MANAGEMENT

CATALOGING AND CLASSIFICATION

The cataloging and classification of videocassettes should be a given in any library collection. This is true whether the collection is in a separate department or interfiled with the book collection. It is also true even if the collection is small. It is essential that the material in the collection be accessible to library users. It is also a given that without careful planning and implementation this issue can cause headaches and strife, particularly between the technical services department and the public service area.

There are some aspects of videocassette cataloging that are exactly the same as for the book collection, and some that can be frustratingly different. First and foremost, the primary consideration should be the library user. Therefore, the best solution to cataloging and classifying the video collection is that libraries should employ the same classification and subject heading scheme they use for the book collection. If the book collection uses the Library of Congress system, so should the video collection. This way, library users can consult the main catalog and find video materials listed along with print materials on any given subject. The civil rights movement? "Eyes On the Prize" should be found in the catalog along with *One More River To Cross*. Simple subject headings are also important. There is a popular misconception that a public library popular collection doesn't need this expensive process. A librarian I know tells a cautionary tale. Her library intended to have only a "browsing collection" of video. Her decision was to put a simple accession number on each video, and list them by title. This works well with feature films, but as "how-tos" and other nonfiction titles were added it turned into a nightmare. A user asking for a video on Chinese cooking had to depend on the librarian to remember the first word in titles on Chinese cooking.

While at first glance formal descriptive cataloging might seem an unnecessary expense, some simple cataloging will save time and money over the long haul. Admittedly, problems can arise because the cataloging of videocassettes is different from the cataloging of books. For one thing, the title, rather than the author, is the main entry. It is also true that the videocassette is more difficult to handle. There isn't an index to consult to get an idea of the contents. Browsing is difficult. Also, credits can be much more difficult to decipher, with more possible entries to consider, than the straightforward title page of a book. For example, while the "author" is usually the producer and/or director (already judgment calls to be made), there are others to be considered for subject tracings; e.g., screenplay, cinematography, editing. In feature films actors can be important, as well as costume designer, art director, etc.

The library staff needs to decide how extensive the cataloging should be for the collection, and then move to accomplish this in the most efficient manner. This might not be on-site cataloging. For the public library, complete tracings for film titles may not be necessary. If the library has a large and serious cinema research collection, then complete credit tracings are probably necessary. For most collections, it is the subject content in nonfiction titles that will be the most important. Academic libraries supporting a cinema studies department will, of course, need complete tracings.

Libraries subscribing to OCLC can get a great deal of information from this service. Problems can arise, however, in having to wait for the information on new titles. Unfortunately, the Library of Congress has stopped the cataloging of all video titles, though even when they offered this service the time lag always made this an unsatisfactory source for cataloging newer titles.

For a public library with a small collection and a technical services department on site, it is possible to find information on some titles in library review sources. *Booklist*, for example, provides simple, professionally produced cataloging information. The disadvantage, of course, is that this information is limited to titles reviewed in this journal.

Another good choice is to purchase cataloging services. Both Baker & Taylor and Ingram will provide cataloging service for titles purchased from them. Another source is Professional Media Service (19122 S. Vermont Ave., Gardena, CA 90248). This vendor not only provides complete cataloging for video titles, but also offers a retrospective cataloging service for titles already owned. This, however, is a fairly expensive proposition. Better by far to catalog from the beginning, though this advice, given at this point in time, does smack of shutting the barn door after "Black Beauty" has fled. There is also help available in professional literature, both on the direction to take with cataloging the video collection, and with the cataloging itself. Some good sources appear at the end of this chapter.

A Few Movies Featuring Libraries and Librarians

Breakfast at Tiffany's
Everyone remembers the scenes of Audrey Hepburn looking in the Tiffany windows, but remember those wonderful scenes in the NYPL reading room where she was researching millionaires? Directed by Blake Edwards, 1961.

Desk Set
This may have been about a room-sized computer, but the story of machines replacing librarians seems very current. But then, this was released in 1957, and we're still here. Directed by Walter Lang, starring Tracy and Hepburn. 1957.

Foul Play
An amusing action/comedy featuring Chevy Chase and Goldie Hawn as a very hip and lively San Francisco librarian. Directed by Colin Higgins, 1978.

Ghostbusters
Nostalgic for the card catalog? Watch one fly in a thousand directions—and get slimed. Directed by Ivan Reitman, 1984.

It's a Wonderful Life
It's hard to love a movie, no matter how beloved, that portrays being the town librarian as the heroine's worst nightmare. Directed by Frank Capra, 1946.

Goodbye, Columbus
Richard Benjamin is the angst-ridden young librarian in this adaptation of Philip Roth's novel. Directed by Larry Peerce, 1969.

The Music Man
Who can forget the musical that gave us "Marian the Librarian," not to mention a splendid library production number. Directed by Morton DaCosta, 1962.

Shadow of a Doubt
Library research can be dangerous when you are a character in an Alfred Hitchcock thriller. Directed by Alfred Hitchcock, 1943.

PACKAGING

"Marketing" is an important part of library service. One may not be able to tell a book by its cover, but there is no question that one is more likely to try a book with an attractive jacket. This phenomenon of human nature is just as true for video. So, while sturdiness and ease of handling are very important, it is equally important to offer appealing packages. Most video distributors now understand this. Virtually all programs purchased commercially will have color cover art, with a description of the program inside. The days of plain black boxes denoting "serious" programming are mercifully just about over.

Another advantage to purchasing the usually higher-priced programs from educational and independent distributors is that they usually come in sturdy boxes, while most home video must be repackaged before circulation. The cardboard sleeves provided by most producers (with some notable exceptions, such as Disney) last just about as long as you think they would. Be sure, however, to keep that original cover for the information provided there.

To solve this problem, libraries can house home videos in higher-quality boxes. Just about all library supply companies now sell sturdy boxes, as do video business suppliers. By purchasing in quantity the library can minimize this added expense. Most plastic cases now come with a clear sleeve so that original box art can be easily transferred, thus keeping the attractiveness of the original, while providing longevity. These boxes also provide a better base for other library necessitates, such as property stamps, classification numbers, bar codes, etc. All of this, of course, costs money in terms of supplies and staff time. Most school, academic, and special libraries do not have these same considerations, except for the need to provide sturdier boxes for home video titles.

SHELVING AND DISPLAY

Closely related to the packaging issue is that of the housing of the videos and their display. Most public libraries have now abandoned the initially popular "two-box" system. With this system, empty video packages were put on display (like most video stores). A borrower would bring the box to the video department or main circulation desk and would then be given the video in a separate box. An alternative method had the video boxes flattened and displayed in thin plastic sleeves. This, of course, saved lots of space.

The problem with these systems is easy to spot. First, with most libraries struggling with space problems, video materials demanded double space—one for storage and one for display. Also, these systems are very labor-intensive, in that library staff has to stop to retrieve the material for the borrower. The reason libraries did this was, of course, security. However, many libraries have now found that the two-box system simply isn't worth it in terms of time and space demands.

Where security is a major issue, there is currently a good, if expensive, solution. Many large public libraries are pleased with a new locked video case called Kwik Case, and available from Demco (800-356-1200). This display box can be picked up off the shelf and is designed so that all the box copy can be easily read. However, a special key (kept at the circulation desk) is required for getting to the video itself.

One of the best things about adding video to the library's materials collection is that it doesn't require special storage. While there is some terrific special shelving available, it really isn't necessary for a beginning collection. Video boxes fit quite comfortably on regular library book shelving. Yet, display is important to get the maximum use of the collection. Spine-out video boxes aren't particularly appealing. Here is where a local video emporium can be of assistance. The large national video chains, in particular, are staffed with very sophisticated merchandisers. By visiting an attractive and busy video store it is possible to pick up some good ideas for display.

Some simple suggestions:

- Place at least some of the video titles face out on the shelves. This is a good way to attract attention to the entire collection. Breaking up the display from an endless row of spines sells all kinds of library materials.
- Use all the space available. Low shelving offers the opportunity to display videos on top of the shelves. If the library requires rows of tall shelving, don't forget that the ends of the stacks can be turned into attractive display areas by attaching display shelving.
- As with the book collection, special displays for holidays, special topics of interest, or genres creates interest in the collection. I have noticed in many Blockbuster video stores, for example, a collection of videos featuring the star or director of a currently "hot" title next to the empty space where that "hot" title would be if there were any copies in at the moment.
- A display of staff favorites is an idea that can easily be borrowed from bookstores. Another idea borrowed from video stores is the "changing monthly" display—possibly exercise and diet for January to back up New Year's resolutions, tax preparation and personal finance for April, etc.

In addition to displays, themed lists of recommended videos is a very popular service. These can also be put on bookmark-size paper to help promote the collection outside the video department. One can be slipped into books at the checkout desk.

Of course, all of these displays, simple or complex, call for signs. It is essential in building a serious video collection to clearly label classification sections, subjects, types of videos, etc. Another helpful sign is one that appears on the book shelves to identify videos that tie in with the books. These can be placed on the shelf, or can be made so they slip over the edge of the shelf. They can be as simple as "Visit the video department for videocassettes on this subject;" or they can be more specific "Opera performances on video are available in the video department;" or "*La Traviata* featuring Placido Domingo is available in the video department."

SECURITY SYSTEMS

It is a sad fact of modern life that most libraries of any size find it necessary to employ some type of security system to guard against disappearing materials. It is also a sad fact that videos do have a street value, making them a prime target for disappearing. This is a problem that is particularly serious in large urban libraries. The (somewhat) good news is that the vast majority of libraries don't find video collection shrinkage any larger than any other type of material.

Library security systems are of two types—radio frequency or electromagnetic. The video collection needs to be considered when a library is selecting a system, in that videos can be damaged by the very system that is trying to protect it. In the likely case that a system is already in place, it is essential to be aware of the special considerations for videocassettes: *Magnetic fields used in security systems can damage tapes.*

The solutions are simple:

- use a pass-around system to avoid ever putting tapes through the wear-and-tear of magnetizing and de-magnetizing repeatedly; and
- use the special low-magnetic strips available for videocassettes.

It is also essential that all staff working with circulation be aware of the possible hazards inherent with security systems vis a vis tapes. If there are doubts, check with the security system vendor. They should have information on handling tapes.

STORAGE AND PRESERVATION

While building and maintaining the video collection isn't the terribly expensive and fragile proposition the film collection was, it is still important to take precautions to make videos last as long as possible, especially for the specialized, rare, or out-of-print programs that are in many collections. There are some simple pointers that will help to preserve any video collection.

Some common enemies of videocassettes are:

- extreme heat
- extreme cold
- too much direct sunlight
- dust
- dirty VCR heads
- microwave ovens

Microwave ovens? One librarian told me the story of the seriously melted videocassette returned by a borrower. It seems the household's two-year-old was having a little trouble distinguishing between the VCR and the microwave, so she put a cassette in the oven and turned it on. While not a problem of national proportions, this little tale does effectively make the point that no matter how careful the library is, things will happen. But there are certain precautions that can be taken to guard against most potential problems.

First, some tips on how to handle and store videocassettes while they are in the library building.

- Videocassettes should always be shelved upright, never stacked on their sides.
- While it is better to ask borrowers to rewind tapes for the convenience of the next borrower, it is really preferable to store tapes either at the end of the tape or part way through. This is because videotape stretches, and will do so if stored over a period of time with the weight on the beginning of the reel. This isn't much of a problem for tapes that circulate frequently, such as popular movies, but if the library owns tapes that are valuable and spend extended periods on shelves, it is a good idea to put a policy into practice in which they are not rewound all the way.

- Nothing is worse for videotape than extremes of temperature, especially heat. Borrowers should be encouraged not to leave tapes in car trunks or in closed cars on hot days. Valuable tapes should be kept in cool rooms, and all shelving for videotapes should be away from windows providing extended periods of direct sunlight.
- Dust is a particular enemy of videotape. It can seep into cases if they are exposed to lots of dust, but most often the problem comes from the use of VCRs which haven't been properly maintained. Heads should be cleaned regularly, especially on machines which are used to play borrowed tapes (from libraries and video stores). Head cleaning is really very simple, and kits can be purchased very inexpensively from any electronics store, or even a large drug or variety store. The easiest to use is a cassette that slips into the VCR and cleans as it is run through the heads.

Of course, there is no way to police borrowers about the condition of the machine they use. It is helpful to put together a short list of hints about VCR and videocassette care as a service to borrowers. This can be made available at the circulation desk. It is a good idea to include some type of tactful statement about the library not being responsible for damage. A surprising number of people blame the tape for "ruining my machine." This is very unlikely in the case of a well-maintained VCR.

What about the care of the video collection itself? The extent of maintenance and repair to the collection will vary depending on the purpose of the collection. If the collection is largely low-cost popular home video the library won't want to spend too much time and money on maintenance. A tape that cost only $9.95 in the first place is cheaper to replace with a new copy than to spend staff time inspecting and repairing. On the other hand, if the collection has rare, special, and expensive programs, care and maintenance are a saving in the long run.

How long should a videotape be expected to last? Well, if a new tape is in the hands of the two-year-old with the microwave oven, it could be only one circulation. At the other end of the spectrum, a video on a specialized subject that isn't circulated very often could last for many years. A caution: the promises of the early days of video claiming that videocassettes would last indefinitely have turned out to be false. Yet most libraries with a number of years of experience to call on report that videos probably last, on average, about 300 circulations.

In the days of 16mm film collections, one of the most time-consuming and expensive aspects of the service was that each film had to be cleaned and inspected each time it circulated. Thank heaven video freed us from that particular headache, but if the collection contains material beyond the $19.95 range (which we hope it does), some cleaning and inspection can be valuable in extending the life and look of the collection. Machines are available that do this quickly and effectively. They come in various price ranges and levels of sophistication, though it seems that if the library is going to make the investment of time to do the cleaning and inspecting, it is a good idea to purchase good institutional equipment. An audiovisual equipment dealer should be able to advise you on this type of machinery.

What about the repair of damaged videocassettes? Yes, it is possible, and not even that complex. However, the question should be viewed in the context of the cost of the repair against the cost of replacement. Repairs are worth it for expensive programs, for those that are no longer available on the market (and are deemed worth replacing), as well as for one part of a series, when the rest of the series is in good condition. Remember, too, that many companies, especially in the educational field, will make special deals for replacing cassettes.

Probably the most common repair that is easy to accomplish is the broken tape. It is relatively simple to remove the outside shell and splice the break, using special material readily available from video suppliers. You will need a special screwdriver, but often screws, spindles, etc., can be collected off cassettes that are being discarded. This type of task is often easily handled by student workers or library volunteers. A good solution for a small library with limited staff is to contract with either a local video store or the local school district for inspection and repair service.

DEACCESSION

In maintaining a quality video collection, it is just as important to know when to remove programs as when to add them. The library's overall policies on collection weeding will work well for many of the decisions about the video collection, as well. For example, shabby packaging is a good reason to remove something from the shelf. Keeping the collection attractive does much to encourage its circulation. If a videocassette is still in good shape, the package can be changed. This is particularly true if the original box art has been maintained inside a plastic slipcase. When the art work has been damaged libraries have employed various methods for dealing with the problem—some have used a copy machine to copy the art, though the lack of color in most cases certainly detracts from its appeal. Yet this method does have the advantage of preserving the copy and design of the cover art. Still others use the method of designing some type of attractive generic cover. By adding information about the video inside this can work reasonably well if all else fails. The worst solution is the plain black box. While practical and inexpensive, this is the kiss of death for even the liveliest video.

As to the program itself, nothing is more important to maintaining a quality video collection than to keep the tapes themselves in good condition. As mentioned before, many of us hoped that the advent of video would mean years of pristine picture and sound quality. Sadly, this is not the case. Videos deteriorate and need to be discarded, just like 16mm films, not to mention books. Commonly the wear-and-tear shows up in the form of scratches in the picture. While very often the band of white scratches appearing across the middle of the screen can be eliminated by the use of the tracking dial on the VCR, as a video wears out it will begin to look scratchy. When this happens it is time for replacement. The other common problem is with the stretched tape, which leads to a distorted soundtrack. When these problems occur they should be treated in the same manner as stained pages, inked underlining, and the like. Time for the heave-ho, painful as that may be.

Of course, a problem for librarians is that damaged videocassettes are more difficult to identify than damaged books. You usually can't tell by looking at them. It is a good idea to have the video collection users assist with this. Either in the video box, or in a prominent place near the circulation area, the library should provide a simple form for the reporting of damage. Just the title and the nature of the damage (and how far into the tape it occurs) should be sufficient. These tapes can then be set aside for inspection and repair before being returned to the circulating collection or discarded.

Certainly it is also important to keep track of the currency of information and weed out outdated material. Good video programs, like good books, stand the test of time. There are classics, both in the feature film and documentary categories, that should never leave the collection. But the collection should be on a regular schedule for review. This can be part of whatever system the library uses for review of the print collection, and is often tied to subject areas.

There are some considerations that are similar to the book collection, and some are quite different.

- Outdated information. This, as with the print collection, is of vital importance. Almost every subject area has some aspects that call for updating. New information in the scientific community, for example, needs to be added and superseded information withdrawn. New perspectives on historical events need to be reflected. Most important, videos in the health area need to be reviewed on a very regular basis, and new information must be added, and outmoded information removed. An example is in the field of AIDS research. Over the ten years that AIDS has been in the forefront of American consciousness and concern, the information has changed drastically. This can be of life-and-death importance, as can so much of the health information available over the library's entire collection.
- Outdated style. While no one would suggest the removal of *Casablanca* because the clothes and ideas are outmoded, certain materials of not quite so classic mien should be removed. Filmmaking, like literary style, changes. Particularly in the nonfiction collection, such material as travelogues can appear terribly dated because of cars, clothing, and even attitudes, not to mention the changing face of cities, etc. This becomes of particular importance in the choice of young people's materials. Essential information can be totally dismissed if a program features kids who are sporting outmoded clothing and haircuts and using outdated language.

So, in summary, the video collection needs to be reviewed on a continuous basis for physical damage both to the packaging and the videotapes themselves; and on a regular basis for currency of look and information. (See the Appendix for "Evaluating Library Collections: An Interpretation of the Library Bill of Rights.")

PROCESSING

So far throughout this work we have referred in various ways to how a videocassette is acquired and then circulated to the user. It might be useful to spend a little time discussing just what considerations there are in getting from one end of the processing spectrum to the other.

- Title. Unlike the book business, the video business is not consistent in matching the title on the cover with the title inside. Particularly with home video titles, which often change distributors, the practice has sometimes been to give an old video a new title to extend its sales life. This, of course, can drive technical processing staff to distraction. Efforts by librarians working with the video industry are improving the situation, but it is always a good idea, if the library is doing its own processing, to check to be sure the titles match.

- It is also a good idea to check tapes (as much as possible) for physical defects. For a busy staff this may not be feasible, certainly, but it is the optimum. With some inexpensive tapes, once the cellophane has been removed, it cannot be returned. This is not a problem with the educational companies, and if the library is dealing with a major library supplier, this should also not be a problem. Another consideration that is not apparent from information on the video box, is what material has been added to the tape. Some companies have taken to adding previews of coming attractions at the beginning of feature film videos. While there's really not anything to be done about this, some libraries have found family films that contain previews for some very sophisticated movies. While libraries won't want to censor a video on this basis, in some situations it is valuable information to have.

- In processing a new video for circulation, the library will want to be sure to have ample library identification on the cassette itself, and on the box. In addition to an ID stamp, it is a good idea to add some other subtle identification, such as a felt-tip pen dot in the spindle bay of the video. Sometimes someone will make a dubbed copy of a library tape and return the dubbed copy, keeping the original.

- Before placing a video on the shelf, the following are certain (mostly obvious) steps to be taken.

- Switching the videocassette and its package art to a sturdy case, if needed.
- Providing cataloging and classification both on the videocassette and in the library's catalog.
- Adding security strips and bar codes, if used. Remember to purchase low-intensity magnetic strips to avoid damaging the videotape.
- If the library is not using an automated circulation system, adding a card and pocket inside the case.

MARKETING THE COLLECTION

Once the videocassettes are cataloged, processed, and displayed on shelves there is still one step to accomplish—letting the world know that the collection is there. In the early days libraries pretty much found that promotion of the video collection was gilding the lily. The users were anxious to use the collection, and demand often outstripped the library's resources, resulting in empty shelves. It therefore may seem like an unnecessary expenditure of time to promote the already popular collection.

Yet it is my guess that, as with the book collection, not all segments of the video collection are being used equally. While most people know to come to the library to get mainstream movies, fewer have any idea of the treasures that are buried in the rest of the collection. The resulting satisfied users and increased circulation figures make promotion of the collection a worthy effort.

This is why simple efforts like signs can be useful. Opera lovers in the book stacks should be informed that there are opera videos available, too. Even signs in the video collection itself can help. Readable labels on sections of the shelving for "World War II," "Children's Stories," "Gardening," and "Travel in Europe" can help people find items they didn't know they were looking for, as well as items they came to find.

One librarian I know uses Friday afternoons as promotion time. Many public libraries find that the shelves empty of popular feature films very early on Friday afternoon. This clever librarian asks frustrated borrowers what they came to find and then suggests really good nonfiction videos as substitutes. Nonfiction circulation has gone up dramatically at her library. Special subject and seasonal displays are pretty hackneyed, but also very effective. Lessons learned through experience with book displays can come in handy here, too. And mixing books, audio, and video in these subject displays is an appreciated public service. Newspaper publicity about those videos, from documentaries about issues of high interest to the library's constituency, to health issues and how-tos and arts can help build the library's accessibility and visibility in the community.

Another tried-and-true library community service is the public program, whether it is story hour or a series for seniors. People still like to get together for a shared experience, especially if discussion is attached. So, just because people are able to look at programs at home, this doesn't mean library programs are no longer needed. In fact, many libraries are finding that public programs are more popular than ever. Whether it's social issues, armchair travel, or story hour, programming is a valued service in many communities.

All of this is, of course, "preaching to the choir"; or those who are already inside the library. Building bridges to the community with the video collection can be very rewarding. One of the wonderful results of the video revolution in libraries is all of the lovely taxpayers who discovered the library for the first time. There are probably still many others who don't think to come to the library for the types of videos they won't find in the local video store.

BIBLIOGRAPHY

Collection Management

Lora, Pat. "When Does a Librarian Need to Think Like a Retailer?" *Wilson Library Bulletin*, January 1992, p. 80.

Pitman, Randy. "The Importance of Being Packaged." *Video Librarian* 6:2, April 1991, pp. 1–4.

Cataloging

Fecko, Mary Beth. *Cataloging Nonbook Resources: A How-To-Do-It Manual for Librarians*. New York, Neal-Schuman, 1993.

Frost, Carolyn O. *Media Access and Organization: A Cataloging and Reference Sources Guide for Nonbook Materials*. Littleton, CO, Libraries Unlimited, 1989.

Handman, Gary. "I Lost It (or Found It) at the Movies: Public Service Implications of Minimal Brief Cataloging of Audiovisual Materials," in *The Video Annual, 1992*, edited by Jean T. Kreamer. Santa Barbara, CA, ABC-Clio.

Intner, Sheila S. "Writing Summary Notes for Films and Videos." *Cataloging and Classification Quarterly* 9:2, 1988, pp. 55–72.
——— and William S. Studwell. *Subject Access to Films and Videos*. Lake Crystal, MN, Soldier Creek Press, 1992.

McCroskey, Marilyn. *Cataloging Nonbook Materials with AACR2 and MARC: A Guide for the School Library Media Specialist*. Chicago, American Library Association, 1994.

Olson, Sharon. *Cataloging Motion Pictures and Videorecordings*. Lake Crystal, MN, Soldier Creek Press, 1991.

Rogers, JoAnn V. and Jerry D. Saye. *Nonprint Cataloging for Multimedia Collections: A Guide Based on AACR2*, 2nd ed. Littleton, CO, Libraries Unlimited, 1987.

Scholtz, James. *Video Acquisitions and Cataloging*. Westport, CT, Greenwood Press, 1995.

6 NEW TECHNOLOGIES AND VIDEO COLLECTIONS

"Don't confuse a clear view with a short distance."
—Paul Saffo, Director, Institute for the Future, speaking at the ALA Midwinter Conference, 1992

Like many of you, I suspect, from time to time I try to picture back to the time when news took several weeks to travel from one side of the country to the other. Ah, the leisure to look at events one at a time, to mull them over, and absorb their impact. This is not a particularly practical wish in these times, when you think that in the time it takes to write this paragraph, events have raced further ahead of me. Or, to bring it into the context of libraries and technology, a friend of mine once opined that while we were standing talking about a new technology, someone in a garage in Japan had probably just invented something that would make the thing we were trying to understand obsolete.

All this to say that trying to sort out the mind-boggling changes in information (read motion picture) delivery is next to impossible. It certainly is impossible using the format of a published book. Since the only certainty is that by the time you would read about this it will be out-of-date, this chapter discusses how libraries can evaluate the changes as they come, and how they might set standards for making decisions about delivery systems.

HOW LONG VIDEO?

One of the dangers in running headlong toward the future is that the world may not be running with us. Thus the quote that opens this chapter. While the library needs to be "cutting-edge" in the sense of not being left behind by other institutions, not to mention the private sector, it really makes no sense to travel too far ahead of the library's constituency. This is particularly true for the public library. While all other types of libraries have a certain control over the timing of choosing and implementing a new format service, the public library must tackle the nearly impossible task of judging where the consumer market is going, and when it will get there. Taking all of that into consideration, it is clear that the 1/2" VHS videocassette is with us for some time to come. It would be a mistake for libraries to assume that because new formats are available there will be a great public demand for them. Remember 8-track cassettes? Or the first introduction of videodiscs in the late 1970s? Or even the *second* introduction of videodiscs? VHS videocassettes will be the *consumer* delivery system of choice for some time to come for the several reasons discussed in the following sections.

UNIVERSALITY

VHS is virtually universal. While there is a regrettable lack of current research on video usage in libraries, the last video service survey conducted reflected a video collection penetration of about 80 percent overall[5]. To all intents and purposes this is a blanket coverage of public libraries if you take into consideration that nearly 50 percent of all public libraries serve a population of less than 10,000.

At the same time, VCR penetration in homes also hovers around the 80 percent mark, and has stayed there for several years. Much of the impression of video being an "old" and tired format comes from a business community that needs us to move on to other machines. The boom days of VCR sales are over. Yet, from the perspective of library public service, this is now a mature and essential part of the library's mandate. It isn't going to disappear overnight in a cloud of electron dust caused by newer and sexier machines.

VIEWING HABITS

Video is how we see many motion pictures. It is sometimes surprising to think how recently we movie lovers had to carefully prioritize our time to get to see movies before they left the theaters. It was a "now or never" proposition. What a gift it has been to be able to pick and choose what we'll spend $7.75 (current going rate in Chicago) to see. Not to mention the scheduling, childcare, and horrific snack prices that are all part of the moviegoing experience.

The videocassette is how many of us see most movies these days. It is certainly the *only* way we see most independents, documentaries, how-tos, etc. Over the next several years that isn't going to change. In the first place, no other format is as satisfactory for the movie-viewing experience, with the huge and notable exception of a theater with a large screen and digital sound. As cineplexes offer smaller and smaller theaters, and home television sets offer larger, sharper pictures and stereo sound, home viewing makes even more sense than it did before.

As this is being written, IBM has just introduced a personal computer with full-screen, full-motion video. This is certainly the next wave, but for the foreseeable future, most people will not be interested in watching a movie on the home computer monitor, and "full-motion" on computers still has the eerie feel of Charlie Chaplin movies projected at the wrong speed.

And above all, there is the "flashing 12:00" syndrome. While the VCR has become exceedingly easy and convenient to use, it is still a mystery to many adults. While most of us can manage to put a cassette in and push "play," even basic recording off the air is beyond most people. My theory is that this is simply the reluctance of many people to take the time to learn something that seems more baffling on the surface than it really is. For these people, all the newer formats appear as more new things to learn. Why change a good thing, i.e., a one-button VCR for seeing a movie?

I think the experience of the videodisc machine confirms this. There is absolutely no doubt that a videodisc is a superior way to see a film. The resolution is beautiful, and multiple tracks make it possible to add interesting material for the viewing experience. Yet the videodisc has resolutely remained the format of movie elitists and technology enthusiasts. It has not been embraced by the general public in large numbers, and with newer formats (the smaller, recordable CD) on the horizon, it looks like it never will be the format of choice.

ECONOMICS

It is not a coincidence that the home video revolution, waiting in the wings for a number of years, happened in the boom times of the mid-1980s. Actually, in some ways the very technological revolution that is making the VCR seem hopelessly out-of-date is prolonging its life. In most households these days, disposable electronics income is going to computers. Yes, CD-ROM with its multimedia capability adds motion to the computer image, but this is not yet a satisfactory medium for narrative programming, as has been discussed above. While home computers have made impressive inroads into society, they are in only 33 percent of the U.S. households[6]. Compare this to the 80 percent for VCRs. Of course these numbers must be taken in context: that 33 percent number is the average; market penetration is higher in affluent communities, and lower in less-affluent neighborhoods.

Industry prognostications were that the year 1995 would see CD-ROM sales double. This is a most impressive gain, and one that indicates this is a format that will be with us for some time to come. But those figures need to be seen in context. While

7,000,000 home computers had multimedia capability at the end of 1994, and 14,000,000 at the end of 1995, this is a relatively small number in the scheme of the entire consumer market. And, for the foreseeable future at least, that CD-ROM figure is really not relevant to the video collection. It is, for better or worse, an *additional* format, much more likely to be used as a reference tool or game platform than as a delivery system for narrative motion pictures.

SLOWNESS OF NEW FORMAT CHANGE

One thing we all know for sure is that at some time in the future the library as we have always known it will disappear. This disappearance will obviously be a gradual process, but the concept of a "library" warehouse for the storage of hard copies of materials will be gone. All materials, not just videocassettes, will be stored in cyberspace, and called down for single use.

In the motion media world we see the beginnings of this transformation in the promise of 500-channel cable delivery and video-on-demand. Video-on-demand, in the context of libraries, will mean that a library user will not have to leave home to acquire a program to view. Two-way communication will make it possible to select a specific program and have it delivered to the home television screen whenever the user wants or needs it. At the same time, the cable (and satellite) industry is promising 500 programmed channels available as widely as our current multiple cable channel offerings. However, there are some glitches in this seemingly attractive picture. For one thing, at least so far, commercial programming imagination does not seem to have expanded with expanded delivery systems. Columnist Ellen Goodman said it best when she wrote of 500-channel cable, "…you will be able to get all the movies you don't want to see anytime you don't want to see them."

In other words, the possibility of niche-market and specialized video programming appearing on expanded cable channels does not appear to be a priority, or even in the pervue of those doing the planning. The curatorial function, as well as the "readers' advisory" role of the librarian is not in much danger of disappearing anytime soon. Add to this the fact that even the basic "movies, movies, movies" of planned 500-channel cable is behind schedule. This is true of those offerings that are to be straight one-way delivery, not to mention the interactive services.

As this is being written the focus is still on the carriers rather than on the services. The "engulf and devour" frenzy of the formation of enormous communications empires is in full swing. The money people are frantically attempting to control both delivery and product—probably an indication that they still don't have a clue as to how all of this is going to play out, either. The struggle among phone companies, cable companies, and satellite delivery companies will also probably go on for some time. Who will control the delivery of motion pictures into libraries and homes? All we know for sure at this time is that two-way interactive full-motion digital delivery *will* happen. And that it isn't going to happen anytime soon for the vast majority of Americans.

Having said all that, I must also say it is essential to keep up with developments, and work with staff, administration, and governing bodies to be sure intelligent decisions will be made when the time does come. We learned from the video revolution that once the waiting is over events can swamp us. I certainly do not envy anyone planning a new library building, for example. Trying to decide what infrastructure will be needed over several decades is not an enviable task. One thing libraries *can* do is ensure they are part of the community planning process. Working with local cable companies, phone companies, and city departments is essential for the library in order to be part of the future community information system.

ADDING A NEW FORMAT TO THE COLLECTION

While it is true that the public library has a more complex and uncertain task in deciding when to add a new service or switch entirely to a new format, all types of libraries can apply certain principles when making such decisions. These principles have been gleaned from the past fits, starts, and actual changes in audiovisual services. Following is a suggested set of considerations for making intelligent and fiscally-responsible decisions about new motion-picture delivery formats for any type of library.

ECONOMY OF SCALE

The underlying principle for any decision about adding a new format is whether there is a combination of population to use the service and sufficient material available to fulfill the demand. While this is most obvious in the case of the public library, most experienced audiovisual professionals in school and academic settings will attest to the "equipment in the closet" syndrome. Sometimes in the past a format was sold to the library but never embraced by the users; or a format was born and then sputtered out before it gained general usage, therefore not enough programming was available for it. There are some simple steps that will help in this regard, though it must be said that it is never foolproof. The best policy is to make the most intelligent choice possible, using all the information available, and work to make the service a success.

Needs Assessment/User Survey. This is a useful technique to use to evaluate any library service, or projected service, but is particularly suited for the addition of new formats. Ask the users if they want it, and in the case of academic institutions, if they are willing to commit the time to learning to use the new format effectively.

In academic libraries, a format may not be of interest to most departments, but is still of such compelling usefulness to some that its purchase is called for. The example that comes to mind is the 12" laserdisc. It is an enormous boon to anyone teaching film study, for example. The random access feature, the pristine technical quality made possible by this format, as well as the extra material (screenplay, director interviews, etc.) added to many releases, make this of tremendous appeal to any film study department.

For the public library, the elusive consumer market must be the primary consideration. Before a new format is added, it is important to find out if it will be used. A survey might ask such questions as what equipment is now owned, what is a possible purchase, and how important is the availability of programming at the library. Choosing who to survey is also key. Surveying only those who are already using library services is certainly essential, but it is also important to find out what might bring new users to the library. This is a lesson many libraries learned with the advent of video collections. This new service vastly extended the reach of local libraries to those taxpayers who had not used library services before. Would the addition of Sega games make an essential contribution to the library's potential constituency? There is no doubt that the line between motion pictures and video games is blurring. Would the addition of video games cause 80 percent of the service population to reach for the smelling salts and vote "no" on the next bond initiative? It is important to know, and then make intelligent choices.

Consumer Trends. The communications industry, as we have discussed, is changing daily, with new formats appearing and disappearing; delivery systems are touted, then abandoned; and everything takes longer than anticipated. However, it is possible to extrapolate useful information from all of the hype. For example, as I stated, in 1995 CD-ROM capability on personal computers jumped from 7 million to 14 million. Additionally, most new personal computers sold with multimedia come with "bundles" of programming, which certainly jump-starts use. Of course, it is equally important to know where these sales are taking place. It is probably of much more importance to affluent suburban libraries in terms of circulating collections. It is of great importance to innercity libraries in terms of purchases to combat the growing threat of information "haves" and "have-nots."

In a time when libraries are having ever greater demands made on budgets that are usually not increasing in a corresponding manner, and in many cases are decreasing, it is also important to look at the new service under consideration in the context of what the library is currently offering and how this new service will add to current services or replace old ones.

FINANCIAL SUPPORT

It is tempting to think that if an exciting new service is offered it will be "discovered," and excitement will lead to utilization. It is a temptation to avoid for a number of reasons. An expensive new service that doesn't find an audience just makes it that much harder to add new services down the line; and, as we have seen, the only sure thing is that there will continue to be new opportunities to add formats and programs. So, while it can be frustrating not to move forward, it is usually worth the extra time and effort to ensure success. As just one example, once a new format is introduced it often dramatically drops in price as it finds its audience. In studying industry projections, does it seem to make fiscal sense to wait six months or a year before making an investment, with the assumption that prices will drop?

Budget approval. Probably no other element is as important for success of a new service as *sufficient* monetary support. This means careful advance study of needs (user survey); a realistic assessment of costs; and a carefully crafted evaluation of benefits. All of this material needs to be presented to the library's administration and governing body in a way that makes the decision clear and easy, and with no surprises.

In formulating the budget it is important to be realistic about all of the costs. These might include:

- programs (software). In the case of video, for example, there was and continues to be the disparity in price between mainstream entertainment fare and specialized educational and alternative/independent materials. Based on the library's mission, it is important to make budget requests for programming considering what types of programs will be purchased, and in what quantity.

- hardware (machinery to run the programs). This is an extremely important consideration for school and academic libraries because the purchase price of hardware to run a format very likely outstrips the costs of the programming for it. Because of these potentially large expenditures, it is critical to establish keen interest in faculty for the format under consideration. It is the threat of the nightmare of the machines in the closet again.

While it is not necessary to offer machines to run videocassettes as part of the public library's video service (though many libraries do), there are still equipment considerations. Damaged tapes need to be inspected, staff needs to be able to evaluate content, and most libraries want to present some types of programs. Additionally, with new formats, it is increasingly important to consider whether the library has an obligation to make this service available in the library for those who do not have access to it personally.

Staff and Training. Another cautionary lesson learned by many during the video "revolution" was that it is of utmost importance to keep the staff, especially those dealing directly with the public, thoroughly informed about all decisions made about the video service; and to include as many of them as possible in making decisions relating to the service. How many times in the early days of video frenzy in the public library did we hear staff refer to being annoyed by video borrowers, who were using up time that should be spent on "real" library users?

This investment in staff takes a couple of forms. First, the budget for a new service needs to include sufficient staff hours to handle the implementation and maintenance of the service. If the library is fortunate and the new service is a big hit, it is important to be able to add staff for support. Second, it is important to train staff in advance. Everyone who will be involved with the new service in any way should have the opportunity to learn about the new service; why it is important, what the library is trying to accomplish by offering the service, and very importantly, hands-on experience in operating machinery and using the programming.

The budget needs to allow for training costs and staff time, both for introduction and for implementation and maintenance.

Product. In considering a new format it is important to ask how much programming is available and what type of programming it is. In other words, does the available material fit the library's mission?

Sufficiency. The first product consideration is sufficiency. Very often hardware developers and programming providers are very far apart. A new piece of machinery or a new delivery system may have enormous potential, but when it is introduced it almost never has enough appropriate programming. Glitzy "demo" programs only show what a product can do, not what is already available or what *should* be available.

Appropriateness for the library's mission is an important consideration. Taking motion pictures as a whole, there are currently a number of delivery systems available, and not all libraries will make the same decision about formats. For example, an academic library with an active film studies program will most likely want to offer a film collection on videodisc because of technical quality and random access features. On the other hand, a public library serving a general population with a popular movie collection would be most likely to offer VHS videocassettes, since that is the overwhelming delivery system of choice in the consumer market. The choice has nothing to do with the quality of the format, and everything to do with supply and demand. While other formats may be technologically superior, you can't beat VHS for availability of a variety of material.

Quality. Another product concern is the quality of the programming that is available. This has two aspects: the quality of the programming offered, and the quality of the presentation. For example, 8mm video is available on the consumer market, and has been for some time. While the audio-sized cassettes and small players are very appealing, there are a couple of problems. First, consumer demand has not built to the point where anything but the most popular and mainstream movies are available for sale. The other is that looking at a movie on that tiny little screen may be a novelty, but not a very satisfactory viewing experience. Yes, it is possible to hook it up to your television set for a larger image, but this does not satisfy the problem of paucity of good programs.

Not meaning to beat up on this one format, I admit to a terrible bias against teeny little screens. They remind me of that curiosity of my childhood, the 1" square Bible. If you used a magnifying glass you could see that the entire Bible was there, but it certainly didn't allow for actual reading of the text. Looking at *Lawrence of Arabia* on a 2" screen strikes me as a similarly unenlightening experience.

In other words, it is important to look at the entire picture of what the library users need, and what a new format is able to offer in the realm of programming that helps fulfill the library's mission, before deciding to add a new service.

EQUIPMENT

As with programming, it is very important to consider equipment needs when adding a new format or service. Availability and service are of equal importance in making these decisions.

Availability. First, is equipment to run this new format readily available to the library and to the user? While it can be annoying to purchase a program from a source and then not be able to replace it because the company has gone out of business, it can be an extremely expensive disaster in the case of hardware. If the library is testing a new format on a limited basis there is not much risk, and much can be learned. But if the time has come to move into a new format full-tilt, it is essential to have confidence that the equipment will not disappear in a year. This can be another of the dreaded "equipment-in-the-closet" phenomena.

One way to avoid this problem (though nothing is foolproof) is to work closely with an audiovisual equipment distributor that you learn to trust. These companies offer a full line of equipment to run all types of audiovisual programs, and offer maintenance and service on the equipment, as well. Libraries can also negotiate good prices on quantity orders. These dealers can be a godsend to the librarian with limited knowledge of the machines and how they work. A good one will also be able to assist with the decision about when a new format has gained sufficient momentum to suggest a certain amount of stability.

Service. The issue of service is closely related to the issue of availability. No matter how wonderful a format or service may be, the law of audiovisual service dictates that the machines will wear out, break, and/or have assorted mysterious "fits." It is also true that they can be very expensive to fix. These are important considerations when planning a new service.

As discussed above, it is imperative to have a resource for servicing the equipment. In addition to having a service contract, dealers will also be able to sell and service institutional-type equipment. While at first blush it might seem tempting for a library to purchase the often-cheaper consumer models of audiovisual hardware, this is usually in the "penny-wise and pound-foolish" category. Machinery in libraries is usually used by a number of people with varying degrees of expertise and respect for the equipment. It is often moved around and is sure to get heavy use. In the long run it pays to purchase the initially more expensive institutional models, especially considering that using an institutional dealer will also provide you with a source for help and spare parts.

So, determining factors in considering any new audiovisual format are:

- what is needed to run it (both equipment and programming)?
- how much will it cost?
- is it readily available from a reliable source?
- can it be easily replaced, maintained, and repaired?

COLLECTION USE

It is all very well to be on the cutting edge by offering a new format, but it is pointless if the library's constituency is not ready to make use of the materials offered. There are a couple of strategies to use in trying to insure success—evaluating and learning from the constituency's history of embracing the new, and the marketing of the new service once it is in place.

History of Support. Does the library's constituency have a history of supporting new formats? A good indication of what the users want will, of course, be the results of the surveys the library takes. Yet, nothing is as telling as looking at the facts about new format adoptions in the past. At what point did the library's borrowers use the video collection in large numbers? Was the collection a result of user demand? Or did the library make the decision to offer the service and then have usage build slowly? This history, especially about videocassettes, can be essential to making intelligent decisions about when to add a new motion media format to the library's services.

This decision is very much a local one. For example, a few years ago, when videodiscs were first appearing on the market, I led a workshop for a group of public libraries on video collection development, part of which was about new technologies on the horizon. When I was cautious about the videodisc format, one librarian offered the information that her community was surveyed and more than 50 percent had videodisc capability at home. It took me a few minutes to get the point—these were public libraries located in the Silicon Valley region of California. Should they invest in videodiscs? Absolutely.

Usage. How will the library guarantee usage of the new collection? In the day-to-day struggle to keep your head above water, it is easy to forget that in addition to other efforts with a new format or service, it is important to be sure the constituency knows about its availability. In academic settings, this can be handled effectively through in-house notification of potentially-interested faculty, and in formalized training in the materials and the use of the equipment needed to utilize the materials. This last is key. None of us likes to be in the position of trying to make a presentation when we aren't confident in the smooth running of the av components.

For the public library it is important to let the community know that the new service is available and to encourage its use. In-house and newspaper/newsletter publicity is very important. It is equally important to understand the most effective timing for the publicity. If there is already a demonstrated demand for the service, and if the library is starting small, it might be a good idea to have a publicity-free "shakedown" period before widespread publicity. The only thing worse than no demand is too much demand when a service is new. The frustration of finding nothing available can drive people away for good.

This is a very important point that overarches everything about a new service. *Don't offer more than can be delivered.* Once it is clear the library wants to offer this new motion media service, and the plan and budget have been adopted, it is almost always a good idea to run a test. Offering service for a time in one school or one library branch will pay off in the long run. Expectations won't be built up and not be able to be fulfilled, the inevitable bugs can be worked out, and perhaps most importantly, staff will have time to learn the new service and feel comfortable with it.

CONCLUSION

As I have stated a number of times, our field has always been subject to change, and now it is changing faster than ever before. During the time I have been writing this book, things have changed. What a strange year that began with the President of the United States opening the State of the Union address with the "v-chip." This is the most important issue to be discussed in the most important Presidential speech of the year? The "v-chip" and all its attendant rhetoric will likely have some impact on libraries. Though on the surface it is about homes and broadcast television, the bandwagon effect created by the discussion of "protecting" children from the evils of Hollywood will inevitably spill over to pre-recorded videocassettes. This is a good time to be sure library access policies are clearly in writing, and all staff are comfortable with those policies and the procedures that should accompany them.

Also, this is the year of the Telecommunications Act. The implications are enormous for libraries, from the good (access to electronic information for everyone), to the chilling (the possibility of library responsibility for child access to "harmful" sites on the Internet). It is gratifying to report that the American Library

Association has been pro-active in challenging the anti-access and liability implications in that act.

And, on the hardware front, the digital videodisc is just over the horizon. Will it be the next VHS? Stay tuned.

Whether the delivery system is flammable nitrate film, celluloid, magnetic tape, or electrons hurtling through space, motion pictures in all their forms have found a place in America's libraries as information, as cultural record and as entertainment.

These moving pictures in all their forms will be with us for a long time to come, and libraries will be a storehouse and guide for their use. While we have spent a lot of time talking about the details, the big picture remains the same—libraries and motion pictures belong together. As the great visual media master, Bill Moyers, said at a PLA conference several years ago, "There are bad books and good books. There is bad television and good television. Good books and good television ought to be good neighbors, each concerned not only with the art of pleasure but with the art of truth. The enemy of both is mediocrity."[7]

Network!

ALA's Video Round Table sponsors two excellent electronic sources for librarians concerned with video collections. VIDEOLIB is a lively discussion vehicle on video collections in libraries. It has proved particularly helpful for reference inquiries and the location of specific video titles. It also acts as a forum for serious and spirited discussion of copyright, access and other issues.

VIDEONEWS is a source for learning about new video titles coming on the market, and is the opportunity for distributors to get the word out about new releases quickly and efficiently.

To subscribe to VIDEOLIB or VIDEONEWS, send an e-mail message:

TO: lisproc@library.berkeley.edu
SUBJECT: leave blank
In the body of the message, type: SUB VIDEOLIB or SUB VIDEONEWS [your first name, last name].
You will receive an acknowledgment and instructions.

Inquiries to:
Gary Handman, Director
Media Resources Center
Moffitt Library
UC Berkeley
(ghandman@library.berkeley.edu)

BIBLIOGRAPHY

Barlow, John Perry. "The Economy of Ideas: A Framework for Rethinking Patents and Copyrights in the Digital Age (Everything You Know About Intellectual Property is Wrong)." *Wired*, March 1994, pp. 5–12.

Bender, Ivan. "Copyright Law and the Newer Technologies." *Wilson Library Bulletin* 67:10, June 1993, pp. 44–47.

Kapor, Mitchell. "Where is the Digital Highway Really Heading? The Case for a Jeffersonian Information Policy." *Wired* 1:3, July-August 1993, p. 53.

Lubedski, Greg W. "Multimedia To Go: Circulating CD-ROMs at Geauga County Public Library." *Library Journal*, February 1, 1995, pp. 37–39.

Rosen, David. "Fiber Optics and the Future of Television." *NVR Reports*, Winter 1991.

Sapadin, Lawrence. " Intellectual Property in a Multimedia Environment." *NVR Reports*, March 1995.

St. Lifer, Evan. "Catching On to the 'Now' Medium: LJ's Multimedia/Technology Survey." *Library Journal*, February 1, 1995, pp. 44–45.

APPENDIX 1:
BOOKLIST CRITERIA FOR EVALUATING NONPRINT MATERIALS

The following criteria are designed as guidelines for use by *Booklist*'s field reviewers in their evaluation of various types of nonprint materials. All of the criteria will not apply to each item evaluated, e.g., visual criteria are not applicable for sound recordings, but the following topics offer both general and specific criteria by which materials may be judged.

Authenticity

Is it authentic, accurate and up-to-date?
Is it free from bias, prejudice or misleading emphasis?
Is the author or producer well qualified?
Are translations and retellings faithful to the original?

Utilization

Will it stimulate and maintain the user's interest?
Will the user be stimulated to further study or discussion?
Is it useful with individuals as well as groups?
Are the format, vocabulary, concepts and rate and methods of development appropriate for the intended audience?
Will it develop concepts that are difficult to get across in other ways?
Will it affect attitudes, build appreciation, develop critical thinking or entertain?
Does it achieve its stated purpose?

Content

Is it well organized and well balanced?
Is the script well written and imaginative?
Is it timely or pertinent to library, community or curriculum needs and problems?
Is the treatment, e.g., animation, dramatization, illustrated lecture, factual analysis, etc., appropriate for the subject?
Does it present information in ways that other materials do not?
Does it complement printed or other audiovisual materials in the same subject areas?
Could the subject be treated better by other media?

Technical Qualities

Is the photography, e.g., choice and handling of visuals, composition, color, focus, exposure, special effects, etc., satisfactory and effective?

Are the visuals other than photographs, e.g., paintings, illustrations, maps, charts, etc., well reproduced and effectively used?

Are the principles of artistic balance and design observed?

Are titles, captions and explanations readable and of suitable length and in proper position?

Is the sound acceptable, e.g., good fidelity, realistic sound effects, synchronization and absence of conflicts between the background music or sound effects and the narration or dialogue?

Is the editing, e.g., continuity, matching, rhythm, pacing, etc., satisfactory?

Do the actors have good voice quality, diction and timing?

Is the acting believable and convincing?

Does the narrator have good voice quality, diction and timing?

Is the narrator condescending in mannerisms and style?

Overall Rating

(In addition to the above criteria the following general criteria should be considered when giving the item an overall rating.)

Is the production imaginative and creative?

Is it of significant educational, social or artistic value?

Is it worth the purchase price?

Are accompanying guides or notes well written and helpful?

Is the packaging easily manipulated and durable?

© Booklist. Printed by permission.

APPENDIX 2: MODEL VIDEO EVALUATION FORM

Title:

Running Time: Release Date:

Producer:

Distributor:

Intended Audience:

	5	4	3	2	1	n/a
General Evaluation	5	4	3	2	1	n/a
Structure	5	4	3	2	1	n/a
Clarity of Presentation	5	4	3	2	1	n/a
Performance/Narration	5	4	3	2	1	n/a
Originality/Creativity	5	4	3	2	1	n/a
Production Values	5	4	3	2	1	n/a
Direction	5	4	3	2	1	n/a
Camerawork	5	4	3	2	1	n/a
Editing	5	4	3	2	1	n/a
Sound	5	4	3	2	1	n/a
Graphics/Special Effects	5	4	3	2	1	n/a
Content	5	4	3	2	1	n/a
Accuracy of Information	5	4	3	2	1	n/a
Relevance/Timeliness	5	4	3	2	1	n/a
Thoroughness of Coverage	5	4	3	2	1	n/a
Comparison with Others	5	4	3	2	1	n/a
Suitability for Intended Audience	5	4	3	2	1	n/a
Programming Possibilities	5	4	3	2	1	n/a

Comments:

APPENDIX 3: CONSORTIUM MODELS FOR PURCHASING

In an era of static or shrinking library budgets in the face of ever-increasing demands for new services and choices, the idea of shared purchasing power has great appeal.

The fact is that purchasing cooperatives, consortia, and circuits have long been a mainstay of library audiovisual service. Because of the relatively high cost of 16mm films, many libraries participated in some type of cooperative service in the 1960s and 1970s. While the introduction of low-priced home video in the 1980s had an enormous impact on libraries, specialized and alternative programming has remained relatively expensive, and the above-mentioned increased demand for all types of new services has caused cooperative purchasing to retain its appeal.

In this discussion I will examine in detail three different types of successful consortia, and give specific recommendations for how to establish and maintain a buying consortium.

WESTERN CONNECTICUT LIBRARY COUNCIL (VIDEO CIRCUIT)

The Western Connecticut Library Council consists of public libraries in the western third of Connecticut. It is a traditional library system, offering a number of services, including interlibrary loan. The Council is funded by the Connecticut State Library and member library assessments, with some funds coming from LSCA.

In a circuit, libraries pool funds to purchase a large number of videos at a discount, then divide them into packets and rotate them among members. A fee for membership is established, and a library may buy one or more memberships, to receive one or more packets. Centralized purchasing makes it possible to negotiate favorable prices with suppliers.

In the case of WCLC, there are twenty-four member libraries in the video circuit, and thirty packets of forty-five–fifty titles each. The total collection consists of approximately 2,000 videos, with seventy-five–one hundred titles being added each year. Additionally, each library maintains its own video collection. The libraries are further divided into two circuits for rotating the packets, which switch libraries once a month. In other words, each month a member library receives forty-five to fifty different titles.

Each member library also receives a binder containing lists of the contents of each packet. These lists are updated on a bi-monthly basis. The binder also contains an alphabetical listing of all titles owned by the circuit, and libraries may request interlibrary loan of any title. After the loan is completed, the title reverts to its original packet. Additionally, each packet comes with a contents list so that as a library receives a new packet it can verify that all assigned titles are accounted for. Libraries are charged for missing titles, and they in turn charge the borrower.

Each month one packet rotates into the council's headquarters for maintenance. Outdated material can be pulled, shabby boxes replaced, and tapes inspected and repaired before the packet is returned to circulation. Weeding and addition of new titles to the packets are done on a continuing basis, and all administrative tasks are handled by the Council. These are kept to a bare minimum in order to use most of their funds for the purchase of new titles.

Processing is also kept simple. Each new video is assigned an accession number, and a record is maintained in a simple database. Each video is housed in a sturdy plastic case which allows for the display of the video's original cover art and a 2"x 4" fluorescent sticker identifying it as a circuit video. This label also lists the title, accession number, length, and year of release. Inside the box is a pocket and card. The card is used to do a simple tally of number of circulations. This is the only statistic gathered by the Council. The simple system also allows for the customizing of local circulation procedures—libraries with automated systems create temporary records for the circuit videos.

The circuit is financed by member dues of $450 per year. A library may opt to purchase more than one membership to receive more than one packet. When the circuit was being established, members were assessed a $900 surcharge for start-up costs. Members are invoiced once per year. Also, once a year all members gather, bringing their current packets with them. All the videos are arranged by accession number and an on-the-spot inventory is conducted. Each member is then given new packet lists and each gathers the assigned titles.

This streamlined and economical model works well because of centralized administration. Council staff does all selection, acquisition, processing and maintenance. Problems can arise, of course, when local priorities and procedures clash with group priorities. These potential problems are kept to a minimum here because the circuit purchases popular feature films, classic features, and popular children's titles. This frees local libraries to use the bulk of their video budgets to purchase specialized documentaries, arts, and special interest titles according to local interests. Because of this strategy, savings are realized by purchasing high quality used titles, as well as the circuit being able to take advantage of a state-wide discount from a major supplier of features. The circuit will also occasionally negotiate a discount with a supplier of main-stream documentary programming. Executive Director Tom Lawrence reports that problems have been minimal and usually arise from missing videos and differences in local procedures.

RICHMOND AREA FILM/VIDEO COOPERATIVE (ACADEMIC COOPERATIVE)

The Richmond Area Film/Video Cooperative is a formal standing committee of the Richmond Academic Library Consortium, an organization of twelve colleges and universities in the Richmond-Ashland-Petersburg area of Virginia, offering a number of shared services. The members are both four-year and community colleges, as well a mixture of public and private schools.

The Film/Video Co-op, which actually pre-dated the Consortium, began in 1972 as a 16mm purchasing cooperative. A screening committee previewed and recommended purchase of films which were then shared. This practice stopped in 1983, and then evolved into the present system. The cooperative's purpose is stated as follows in its statement of operational policy and procedures.

a. To assist in making film and video more accessible, to promote its widespread and most effective use, and to recommend optimal standards of service and distribution;

b. to foster cooperative planning and purchasing among the member institutions and the solving of mutual problems;

c. to gather and disseminate information on improved procedures and new developments in media, and to report useful statistics through common reporting forms and terminology;

d. to create and provide staff development programs which benefit the membership;

    e. to produce a union list, to be updated annually, of films and videos owned by the membership;

    f. to shuttle films/videos via van to institutional members for designated loan periods (loan periods are at the discretion of the owner institution.) and

    g. to share the expenses of maintaining such a cooperative venture through annual dues.

Currently all members of the co-op maintain their own media (16mm film, videocassette, and laserdisc) collections, and each year spend an agreed amount for purchase of titles to be shared. Any member institution may book any title listed in the union catalog with the owning institution. The Consortium maintains a four-day-per-week delivery system to all members. All materials borrowed from the Co-op may be used only for educational purposes. Ninety percent of the usage is for classroom instruction.

The Co-op no longer purchases as a group. This part of the operation is much less formal than in the past, but before acquiring an expensive series members will often check with each other. On the other hand, with a series that is in great demand, the institutions tend to purchase their own. The Co-op helps primarily in the area of specialized collections. For example, Virginia Commonwealth University received a special grant for AIDS education, so they buy heavily in that field, leaving other institutions free to purchase in their own specialties, and then share with VCU.

The Richmond Academic Library Consortium is a formal organization, with officers, by-laws, and regular membership meetings. It is financed by members voting on an annual budget, and then dividing by the number of institutions to arrive at annual dues. The Film/Video Co-op, as a standing committee of the Consortium, has its own officers and budget.

It is often the case with shared collections that problems arise out of unequal usage among members. The Richmond group has created a structure for dealing with this issue. Each year statistics are gathered reflecting the borrowing and lending pattern of each individual institution. The number of items borrowed from the co-op the previous year is multiplied by $20. This amount is then used as the requirement for purchasing for the next year of titles that will be shared with the Co-op. In other words, if an institution borrowed 200 items from the Co-op in a given year, the next year it would be required to purchase $4,000 worth of materials ($20 x 200) to be made available to the Co-op. If an institution does not meet its quota for more than one year, its membership is reviewed by the Consortium board. The Co-op has found that this can be a positive for the institution in question because it can help in lobbying administrations to maintain and increase materials budgets. In addition to materials, members may offer in-kind contributions, such as film inspection and catalog production.

While this cooperative is well-established and successful, they do face problems. One is the increasing cost of maintaining a printed union catalog. It currently lists 10,000 titles, and 1,500 more are being added each year. It is an expensive and time-consuming project. While an electronic alternative would be a natural progression, an affordable solution has not been found. Additionally, member institutions have a varying ability to access new technologies. Another problem is the increasing number of programs that are sold with restrictions which make sharing of the material impossible.

NEW YORK STATE PUBLIC LIBRARIES VIDEO CONSORTIUM (STATEWIDE BUYING COOPERATIVE)

In 1990 the New York State Public Libraries Video Consortium was established for the purpose of assisting local libraries in building quality video collections affordably. With this goal in mind, the three founders (Mary Keelan, Mid-Hudson Library System, Delia Gottlieb, Nassau Library System, and Diane Courtney, Westchester Library System), all experienced audiovisual specialists, worked with their directors, the state library, and video distributors to establish the consortium.

The procedures they have evolved attempt to keep bureaucracy at a minimum. Membership in the consortium is available to all twenty-three library systems in the state (743 local libraries). Distributors (largely single source) are invited to submit a proposal for consideration by a selection committee. Basic requirements for submission are that all or a portion of their offerings be made available at a universal price, and that the price be lower than the advertised list price. Public performance rights must be included, and the distributor agrees to bill and ship individually to each institution ordering. Participating library systems, in turn, agree to drop ship catalogs of offerings to all member libraries, organize and affix the consortium stamp to all orders, maintain statistics, and offer advertising through workshops and newsletters, etc.

A limited number of vendors are selected each year by the consortium committee, and a buying window is established. This committee is helpful to local libraries because of members' expertise in visual media; in other words, they can screen vendors for quality programming before it is presented to local libraries, and local librarians can have a high level of confidence in the quality of the offerings.

Administration of the consortium's business is handled by the three systems that founded and organized the group. As with many consortia, problems arise from the amount of time that must be allocated for the consortium, which must be added to already heavy workloads.

A real strength of this organization is its cooperative relationship with vendors. Early success was enhanced by making distributors an integral part of initial planning. A distributor was invited to work with the founders in designing procedures and policies. While this has worked well in New York, care must be taken with this model because vendors are being asked to lower established prices which can lead to other customers demanding equal treatment. Thus, close and open cooperation between vendors and libraries is essential. At the time of this writing, the New York Consortium is operating very successfully, with more than thirty vendor proposals having been submitted for the next buying round.

RECOMMENDATIONS FOR STARTING A COOPERATIVE BUYING GROUP

1. Perhaps the most important element in founding a buying group is dedication on the part of one person or group of people to get it started. As well as a strong sense of purpose, this means a commitment of time, usually on a voluntary basis. This is why it is easier to accomplish through an established entity—library system, state library, or already operating consortium.

   It is also absolutely essential to have the support of the administrations of everyone involved in the establishment and ongoing operation of the group. This support has to be both monetary and in staff time.

2. Another essential is working out policies and procedures that can be supported by all members. Perhaps the most

important is in setting standards for participation (money and resources), so that the issues surrounding equality of use and contribution can be resolved. The consortia that work smoothly all have in common clear rules for participation.

3. In setting policies and procedures it is important to consider local policies that may conflict. Some of these are:

   - interlibrary loan
   - public performance (will videos be used for public programming)
   - charging of fees for borrowing
   - required bidding processes

   While all these considerations can create barriers, they do not necessarily impede group purchasing if the consortium works them out in advance. With issues such as the charging of fees and circulation procedures, the easiest solution is to allow local libraries to use their own procedures.
   In the case of public performance, the consortium must decide whether or not to purchase public performance rights for public programming, and all members must abide by the copyright law on home-use-only tapes.
   As far as bidding processes are concerned, local libraries must work these out with local administrative bodies before joining a group purchasing consortium.

4. Another important consideration for success is working cooperatively with vendors. The group must decide what types of titles will be purchased and then work closely with suppliers. This may take the form of choosing a wholesaler and negotiating a favorable discount for the group, or working with a number of single source distributors to get lower prices on specialized programming. The most successful buying groups treat vendors as partners rather than adversaries.

(This study was made possible by a grant from National Video Resources.)

APPENDIX 4: ESPECIALLY APPLICABLE INTERPRETATIONS OF THE LIBRARY BILL OF RIGHTS

ACCESS FOR CHILDREN AND YOUNG PEOPLE TO VIDEOTAPES AND OTHER NONPRINT FORMATS: AN INTERPRETATION OF THE LIBRARY BILL OF RIGHTS

Library collections of videotapes, motion pictures, and other nonprint formats raise a number of intellectual freedom issues, especially regarding minors.

The interests of young people, like those of adults, are not limited by subject, theme, or level of sophistication. Librarians have a responsibility to ensure young people have access to materials and services that reflect diversity sufficient to meet their needs.

To guide librarians and others in resolving these issues, the American Library Association provides the following guidelines.

The LIBRARY BILL OF RIGHTS says, "A person's right to use a library should not be denied or abridged because of origin, age, background, or views."

ALA's FREE ACCESS TO LIBRARIES FOR MINORS: An Interpretation of the LIBRARY BILL OF RIGHTS states:

"The 'right to use a library' includes use of, and access to, all library materials and services. Thus, practices which allow adults to use some services and materials which are denied to minors abridge use based on age.

> . . . It is the parents—and only parents—who may restrict their children—and only their children—from access to library materials and services. People who would rather their children did not have access to certain materials should so advise their children. The library and its staff are responsible for providing equal access to library materials and services for all library users."

Policies which set minimum age limits for access to videotapes and/or other audiovisual materials and equipment, with or without parental permission, abridge library use for minors. Further, age limits based on the cost of the materials are unacceptable. Unless directly and specifically prohibited by law from circulating certain motion pictures and video productions to minors, librarians should apply the same standards to circulation of these materials as are applied to books and other materials.

Recognizing that libraries cannot act *in loco parentis*, ALA acknowledges and supports the exercise by parents of their responsibility to guide their own children's reading and viewing. Published reviews of films and videotapes and/or reference works which provide information about the content, subject matter, and recommended audiences can be made available in conjunction with nonprint collections to assist parents in guiding their children without implicating the library in censorship. This material may include information provided by video producers and distributors, promotional material on videotape packaging, and Motion Picture Association of America (MPAA) ratings *if they are included on the tape or in the packaging by the original publisher* and/or if they appear in review sources or reference works included in the library's collection. Marking out or removing ratings information from videotape packages constitutes expurgation or censorship.

MPAA and other rating services are private advisory codes and have no legal standing*. For the library to add such ratings to the material if they are not already there, to post a list of such ratings with a collection, or to attempt to enforce such ratings through circulation policies or other procedures constitutes labeling, "an attempt to prejudice attitudes" about the material, and is unacceptable. The application of locally generated ratings schemes intended to provide content warnings to library users is also inconsistent with the LIBRARY BILL OF RIGHTS.

*For information on case law, please contact the ALA Office for Intellectual Freedom.

See also: STATEMENT ON LABELING AND EXPURGATION OF LIBRARY MATERIALS, Interpretations of the LIBRARY BILL OF RIGHTS.

Adopted June 28, 1989, by the ALA Council.

ECONOMIC BARRIERS TO INFORMATION: AN INTERPRETATION OF THE *LIBRARY BILL OF RIGHTS*

A democracy presupposes an informed citizenry. The First Amendment mandates the right of all persons to free expression, and the corollary right to receive the constitutionally protected expression of others. The publicly supported library provides free and equal access to information for all people of the community the library serves. While the roles, goals and objectives of publicly supported libraries may differ, they share this common mission.

The library's essential mission must remain the first consideration for librarians and governing bodies faced with economic pressures and competition for funding.

In support of this mission, the American Library Association has enumerated certain principles of library services in the *Library Bill of Rights*.

PRINCIPLES GOVERNING FINES, FEES, AND USER CHARGES

Article I of the *Library Bill of Rights* states: "Books and other library resources should be provided for the interest, information, and enlightenment of all people of the community the library serves."

Article V of the *Library Bill of Rights* states: "A person's right to use a library should not be denied or abridged because of origin, age, background, or views."

The American Library Association opposes the charging of fees for the provision of information by all libraries and information services that receive their major support from public funds. All information resources that are provided directly or indirectly by the library, regardless of technology, format, or methods of delivery, should be readily, equally and equitably accessible to all library users.

Libraries that adhere to these principles systematically monitor their programs of service for potential barriers to access and strive to eliminate such barriers when they occur. All library policies and procedures, particularly those involving fines, fees, or other user charges, should be scrutinized for potential barriers to access. All services should be designed and implemented with care on a regular basis to ensure that the library's basic mission remains uncompromised.

Librarians and governing bodies should look for alternative models and methods of library administration that minimize distinctions among users based on their economic status or financial condition. They should resist the temptation to impose user fees to alleviate financial pressures, at long term cost to institutional integrity and public confidence in libraries.

Library services that involve the provision of information, regardless of format, technology, or method of delivery, should be made available to all library users on an equal and equitable basis. Charging fees for the use of library collections, services, programs or facilities that were purchased with public funds raises barriers to access. Such fees effectively abridge or deny access for some members of the community because they reinforce distinctions among users based on their ability and willingness to pay.

PRINCIPLES GOVERNING CONDITIONS OF FUNDING

Article II of the *Library Bill of Rights* states: "Materials should not be proscribed or removed because of partisan or doctrinal disapproval."

Article III of the *Library Bill of Rights* states: "Libraries should challenge censorship in the fulfillment of their responsibility to provide information and enlightenment."

Article IV of the *Library Bill of Rights* states: "Libraries should cooperate with all persons and groups concerned with resisting abridgment of free expression and free access to ideas."

The American Library Association opposes any legislative or regulatory attempt to impose content restrictions of library resources, or to limit user access to information, as a condition of funding for publicly supported libraries and information services.

The First Amendment guarantees freedom of expression is violated when the right to receive that expression is subject to arbitrary restrictions based on content.

Librarians and governing bodies should examine carefully any terms or conditions attached to library funding and should oppose attempts to limit through such conditions full and equal access to information because they have an obligation to reject such restrictions when the effect of the restriction is to limit equal access to information.

Librarians and governing bodies should cooperate with all efforts to create a community consensus that publicly supported libraries require funding unfettered by restrictions. Such a consensus supports the library mission to provide the free and unrestricted exchange of information and ideas necessary to a functioning democracy.

The Association's historic position in this regard is stated clearly in a number of Association policies: 50.4 Free Access to Information, 50.9 Financing of Libraries, 51.2 Equal Access to Library Service, 51.3 Intellectual Freedom, 53 Intellectual Freedom Policies, 59.1 Policy Objectives, and 60 Library Services for the Poor.

Adopted by the ALA Council, June 30, 1993.
[ISBN 8389-7702-2]

STATEMENT ON LABELING

An Interpretation of the *Library Bill of Rights*

Labeling is the practice of describing or designating materials by affixing a prejudicial label and/or segregating them by a prejudicial system. The American Library Association opposes these means of predisposing people's attitudes toward library materials for the following reasons.

1. Labeling is an attempt to prejudice attitudes and as such, is a censor's tool.
2. Some find it easy and even proper, according to their ethics, to establish criteria for judging publications as objectionable. However, injustice and ignorance rather than justice and enlightenment result from such practices, and the American Library Association opposes the establishment of such criteria.
3. Libraries do not advocate the ideas found in their collections. The presence of books and other resources in a library does not indicate endorsement of their contents by the library.

A variety of private organizations promulgate ratings systems and/or review materials as a means of advising either their members or the general public concerning their opinions of the contents and suitability or appropriate age for use of certain books, films, recordings, or other materials. For the library to adopt or enforce any of these private systems, to attach such ratings to library materials, to include them in bibliographic records, library catalogs, or other finding aids, or otherwise to endorse them would violate the *Library Bill of Rights*.

While some attempts have been made to adopt these systems into law, the constitutionality of such measures is extremely questionable. If such legislation is passed which applies within a library's jurisdiction, the library should seek competent legal advice concerning its applicability to library operations.

Publishers, industry groups, and distributors sometimes add ratings to material or include them as part of their packaging. Librarians should not endorse such practices. However, removing or obliterating such ratings—if placed there by or with permission of the copyright holder—could constitute expurgation, which is also unacceptable.

The American Library Association opposes efforts which aim at closing any path to knowledge. This statement, however, does not exclude the adoption of organizational schemes designed as directional aids or to facilitate access to materials.

Adopted July 13, 1951. Amended June 25, 1971; July 1, 1981; June 26, 1990, by the ALA Council.
[ISBN 8389-5226-7]

EVALUATING LIBRARY COLLECTIONS

An Interpretation of the *Library Bill of Rights*

The continuous review of library materials is necessary as a means of maintaining an active library collection of current interest to users. In the process, materials may be added and physically deteriorated or obsolete materials may be replaced or removed in accordance with the collection maintenance policy of a given library and the needs of the community it serves. Continued evaluation is closely related to the goals and responsibilities of libraries and is a valuable tool of collection development. This procedure is not to be used as a convenient means to remove materials presumed to be controversial or disapproved of by segments of the community. Such abuse of the evaluation function violates the principles of intellectual freedom and is in opposition to the Preamble and Articles 1 and 2 of the *Library Bill of Rights*, which state:

> The American Library Association affirms that all libraries are forums for information and ideas, and that the following basic policies should guide their services.
>
> 1. Books and other library resources should be provided for the interest, information, and enlightenment of all people of the community the library serves. Materials should not be excluded because of the origin, background, or views of those contributing to their creation.
> 2. Libraries should provide materials and information presenting all points of view on current and historical issues. Materials should not be proscribed or removed because of partisan or doctrinal disapproval.

The American Library Association opposes such "silent censorship" and strongly urges that libraries adopt guidelines setting forth the positive purposes and principles of evaluation of materials in library collections.

Adopted February 2, 1973; amended July 1, 1981, by ALA Council.
[ISBN 8389-5406-5]

APPENDIX 5:
FESTIVALS AND AWARDS

Many wonderful films are never shown at the local multi-screen cinema, or even at art houses. While many appear on public television and through cable, it is easy to miss great material. Following is a list of festivals and showcases for programming appropriate for library collections.

AFI Video Festival
2021 N. Western Ave.
Los Angeles, CA 90027
(213) 856-7707
American Film Institute showcase for independents. Takes place in November.

American Indian Film Festival and Video Exposition
American Indian Film Institute
333 Valencia St., Suite 322
San Francisco, CA 94103
(415) 554-0525
Competitive festival for films by/or about American Indians. Takes place in November.

American Library Association (Association for Library Service to Children)
50 E. Huron St.
Chicago, IL 60611
(312) 280-2162
Notable Films and Videos for Children list appears each January. The Andrew Carnegie Medal for Excellence in Children's Video is awarded in January with the Newbery and Caldecott medals. It is given to the outstanding American children's video of the year.

American Library Association (Young Adult Library Services Association)
50 E. Huron St.
Chicago, IL 60611
(312) 280-4390
Selected Films for Young Adults is selected each January.

Ann Arbor Film Festival
P.O. Box 8232
Ann Arbor, MI 48107
(313) 995-5356
Strong showcase for experimental and film-as-art productions. Takes place in March.

Asian American International Video Festival
Asian Cine Vision
32 E. Broadway
New York, NY 10002
(212) 925-8685
Documentary, experimental, and performance works from Asians and Asian-Americans, with an emphasis on first-time filmmakers. Takes place in April.

Asian Pacific American International Film and Video Festival
Visual Communications
263 S. Los Angeles St.
Los Angeles, CA
(213) 680-4462
Works by Asian-Pacific Americans.

Aspen ShortsFest
P.O. Box 8910
Aspen, CO 81612
(303) 925-6882
Awards in this festival are for the best of productions under thirty minutes. Takes place in February.

Atlanta Film and Video Festival
IMAGE Film/Video Center
75 Bennett St., NW
Atlanta, GA 30309
(404) 352-4225
A festival featuring independents. Takes place in May. Each November there is also the *Atlanta Third World Film Festival*.

Big Muddy Film and Video Festival
Department of Cinema and Photography
Southern Illinois University
Carbondale, IL 62901
(618) 453-1475
Filmmaker juror, featuring all lengths and genres. Takes place in February.

Black Maria Film and Video Festival
c/o Department of Media Arts
Jersey City State College
203 West Side Avenue
Jersey City, NJ 07305
(201) 200-2043
National showcase tour, and a local competition for independents in all formats. Takes place in January.

Charlotte Film and Video Festival
Mint Museum of Art
2730 Randolph Road
Charlotte, NC 20207
(704) 337-2000
Competition for independent and experimental filmmakers in southern states. Takes place in May.

Chicago International Festival of Children's Films
Facets Multimedia
1517 W. Fullerton
Chicago, IL 60614
(312) 281-9075
Well-respected juried festival of animated, live-action, short, and long films for children. Takes place in October.

Chicago International Film Festival
Cinema Chicago
415 N. Dearborn
Chicago, IL 60610-9990
(312) 644-3400
Large juried festival of feature films from around the world. Takes place in October.

Chicago Latino Film and Video Festival
600 S. Michigan Ave.
Chicago, IL 60606
(312) 431-1330
Annual competition for feature films from the United States, Latin America, and Spain. Takes place in September.

Columbus International Film Festival
Film Council of Greater Columbus
5701 N. High St., Suite 204
Columbus, OH 43085
(614) 841-1666
A long-established and respected showcase for educational films and videos. Takes place in October.

Council on International Nontheatrical Events (CINE)
1001 Connecticut Avenue, NW
Washington, DC 20036
(202) 785-1136
The Golden Eagle award has long been recognized from this business/educational group selecting American films to be entered in international festivals.

Dance on Camera Festival
Dance Films Association
1133 Broadway, Room 507
New York, NY 10010
(212) 727-0764
All aspects of performance, biography, experimental, etc. Takes place in March.

Houston International Film Festival
P.O. Box 56566
Houston, TX 77256-6566
(713) 965-9955
The annual Festival of the Americas juries documentary, television, and short films. Takes place in April or May.

International Documentary Awards Film and Video Festival
1551 S. Robertson Blvd.
Los Angeles, CA 90035-4233
(213) 284-8422
Awards given to documentaries by documentary filmmakers themselves. Takes place in November.

International Health and Medical Film Festival
Academy of Medical Films
1601 Ygnacio Valley Rd.
Walnut Creek, CA 94598
(510) 947-5303
Largest competition and showcase for health education and medical films. Takes place in October.

International Women's Film and Video Festival
225 Lafayette St., Suite 212
New York, NY 10012
(212) 925-0606
Women directors, writers, and producers are recognized. Takes place in March.

Miami Film Festival
444 Brickell Ave., Suite 229
Miami, FL 33131
(305) 377-3456
Non-juried showcase of independent film, with a special emphasis on Spanish-language film. Takes place in February.

National Educational Media Festival
655 13th St.
Oakland, CA 94612
(510) 465-6885
A prestigious, judged festival for educational and independent films. Takes place in May.

Native American Film and Video Festival
Museum of the American Indian
Broadway at 155th St.
New York, NY 10032
A showcase of independent productions of all types. Takes place in April.

New Directors/New Films
Film Society of Lincoln Center
Showcase for new filmmakers. Takes place in March.

New York Film Festival
Film Society of Lincoln Center
140 W. 65th St.
New York, NY 10023
(212) 877-1800
Non-juried festival of U.S. premieres of feature films, as well as shorts and documentaries. Takes place in September/October.

Retirement Research Foundation National Media Awards
Center for New Television
1440 N. Dayton
Chicago, IL 60622
(312) 951-6868
The OWL awards are presented to films and videos on issues related to aging. Takes place in May.

San Francisco International Film Festival
1560 Filmore Street
San Francisco, CA 94115
(415) 567-4641
Golden Gate Awards recognize the best in documentaries, television, and shorts. Takes place in April or May.

San Francisco International Lesbian and Gay Film Festival
Frameline
Box 14792
San Francisco, CA 94114
(415) 861-5245
Both showcase and competition for all types of programming by
and about gay men and lesbians. Takes place in June.

Seattle International Film Festival
801 E. Pine St.
Seattle, WA 98122
(206) 324-9998
Features documentaries both from the United States and around
the world. Takes place in May or June.

Washington, DC International Film Festival/Filmfest DC
P.O. Box 21396
Washington, DC 20009
(202) 727-2396
Showcase for nontheatrical productions, as well as restrospective
programs. Noncompetitive. Takes place in April or May.

Women in the Director's Chair Film and Video Festival
3435 N. Sheffield
Chicago, IL 60657
(312) 281-4988
Educational, feature, animated, experimental films directed by
women. Takes place in March.

ENDNOTES

PREFACE

1. Electronic Industry Association. *Electronic Market Databook 1995*. Alexandria, VA, Electronic Industry Association, 1995, p. 19.

CHAPTER 1

2. *Video Source Book*. Gale Research, Detroit. 1995.

CHAPTER 4

3. Reed, Mary Hutchings and Debra Stanek. "Library and Classroom Use of Copyrighted Videotapes and Computer Software." *American Libraries*, February, 1986.

4. Hentoff, Nat. *Chicago Tribune Sunday Magazine*, November 15, 1992, p. 2.

CHAPTER 6

5. Lynch, Mary Jo. *Non-Tax Sources of Revenue for Public Libraries*. Chicago, American Library Association, 1988, p. 14.

6. Electronic Industry Association. *Electronic Market Databook 1995*. Alexandria, VA, Electronic Industry Association, 1995, p. 56.

7. Moyers, Bill. "The Wondrous Power of Television: Video and the Public Library" *Public Libraries*, Fall 1988, p. 118.

INDEX

COLOPHON

Sally Mason-Robinson is a consultant in libraries and the visual media based in Chicago. She is currently project director for the National Video Resources Library Initiative, and recently directed the Video Education for Librarians Project, funded by NVR and the John D. and Catherine T. MacArthur Foundation.

She is the former Director of Video and Special Projects for the American Library Association, Development Consultant to the American Film and Video Association, Director of Marketing for Churchill Films, and Publisher of *Media & Methods* magazine.

She holds an MLS from the University of Southern California, and served as young adult coordinator for the Los Angeles County Public Library, and as audiovisual coordinator for the San Diego County Public Library.

She has been a visiting professor at the University of Washington School of Library and Information Science, and was on the faculty of Columbia University's Children's Literature Institute.

Her articles on video and libraries have appeared in *Library Journal, Sightlines, Wilson Library Bulletin,* and *The Yearbook of Library and Information Services*. She served as co-editor of *Video for Libraries* (ALA, 1988), as a contributing editor to *Video Annual* (ABC-Clio).